Lost Unicorns of the Velvet Revolutions

Lost Unicorns of the Velvet Revolutions

HETEROTOPIAS OF THE SEMINAR

MIGLENA NIKOLCHINA

FORDHAM UNIVERSITY PRESS

New York 2013

Fordham University Press also publishes its books in a variety of electronic formats. Some content that appears in print may not be available in electronic books.

Library of Congress Cataloging-in-Publication Data

Nikolchina, Miglena.
Lost unicorns of the velvet revolutions : heterotopias of the seminar / Miglena Nikolchina. — 1st ed.
p. cm.
Includes bibliographical references and index.
ISBN 978-0-8232-4299-3 (cloth : alk. paper) —
ISBN 978-0-8232-4300-6 (pbk. : alk. paper)
1. Communism—Europe—History—20th century.
2. Communism and intellectuals. I. Title.
HX44.5.N53 2013
335.43094—dc23

2012019757

Printed in the United States of America

15 14 13 5 4 3 2 1

First edition

To Marin, the ever fixed mark in tempests and wandering

Contents

Acknowledgments

This book began at a moment of biographical crisis—which, as I came to see it later, was a splinter from the clash between utopian and available worlds—as a sort of personal letter to a friend, the historian Joan Scott, to whom I wanted to explain what I could not really figure out myself: namely, how I got into this crisis at all. She was the single most important force that helped me persevere in my pursuit of lost unicorns.

Parts of the book were written at the Institute for Advanced Study, Princeton, New Jersey, and at the Institute for the Human Sciences in Vienna, with the support of the Andrew W. Mellon Foundation. I am grateful to Wendy Brown and Elizabeth Weed for their astute comments and to Judith Butler for her crucial intellectual interventions. Discussions with Alenka Zupančič and Mladen Dolar played an important role at later stages of my work. Throughout the years, a lot of inspiration came from talks with Angel Angelov, Alexander Kiossev, Deyan Deyanov, Dimitrina Petrova, Svetlana Subeva, Boyan Manchev, Darin Tenev, and Kamelia Spassova. And finally, my special thanks to Helen Tartar and Thomas Lay, whom I was lucky to meet as my editors.

Introduction

> How often, since there are human beings and human history, have good conversations gone beyond their microcosm and turned into a huge social force! Now close by, now far away, the fires of good conversations are flickering all over the globe today. . . . Conversations are weapons. . . . Nothing was ever done without a good conversation—neither the building of the Parthenon, nor the tearing down of the Bastille.
>
> —Tzvetan Stoyanov, "On Good Conversations"

In her preface to *Between Past and Future*, Hannah Arendt writes, apropos of the French Resistance but also in terms of the history of revolutions per se, of the "lost treasures of the revolutions." One has good reason to believe that these treasures, which seem to have no substance and no name, never existed: "Unicorns and fairy queens seem to possess more reality than the lost treasures of the revolutions." Remembrance, she goes on to say,

> which is only one, though one of the most important, modes of thought, is helpless outside a pre-established framework of reference, and the human mind is only on the rarest occasions capable of retaining something which is altogether unconnected. Thus the first that failed to remember what the treasure was like were precisely those who had possessed it and found it so strange that they did not even know how to name it.[1]

This book is about the unicorns and fairy queens of the East European revolutions. Empirically, its frame of reference will be my own experience of intellectual life in Bulgaria during the 1980s; theoretically, however, it will try to ponder the broader mystery of the treasure that was lost with the very victory over the communist regime. The predominantly oral character of intellectual resistance in the 1980s in Bulgaria—in the mode of what came to be designated as *the* seminar—seems to offer an especially fit parable for the retroactive incapacity to name this loss. We can go back and analyze an incomprehensible text; we can try again and again to decipher the alphabet of a dead language. We cannot really go back to the missing record of what people *spoke*. At best—as noted in a text celebrating the twentieth anniversary of one of the most important 1980s seminars—one could provide the "frugal shorthand denoting an important cultural occurrence. It is, of course, a hypomnema, a recollection mark, some sort of summing up: the textual abstract of a spiritual universe."[2]

The textual abstracts nevertheless keep growing in number and size and raise the question of the type of pull *the* seminar keeps exerting.[3] To begin with, the seminar explicitly valorized dialogue, face-to-face communication, an eroticized togetherness in the sharing of knowledge; in short, it tended to regard the present, the oral, and the unwritten as methodologically superior to the written. Its second obvious aspect was that it was theoretical: Although the seminar would include in its activities anything from poetry readings to art exhibitions and theatrical performances, although it was in itself frequently rather theatrical and performative (as in the case when the ladder of Wittgenstein was literally brought into the seminar room), theory was its lingua franca, its encompassing medium. The third aspect was that the seminar tended to coincide with the life of its participants: This sometimes made it look like a perennial party, but it also implied the idea of the *exemplum*, of the thinker as the embodiment of her thinking in an "existential act." All in all, the seminar was a remarkable phenomenon even if we consider only its steadily accelerating growth throughout the 1980s until it finally metamorphosed into street action and dissolved into the political movements of the early 1990s. So, whatever its role in bringing down the communist regime, its fourth obvious aspect was that it was political.

I believe that the changes in Eastern Europe were an *event*—in Alain Badiou's sense and contrary to Badiou's own assessment of what happened, "as affirmed by all and sundry, that what they think and want, the people of Russia and Hungary and Bulgaria, is nothing other than what already exists."[4] It was an optical illusion—a specular inversion—this impression that the thing all those people wanted already existed. They wanted something else. This something, however, is precisely what was lost. Between Arendt's observation and Badiou's conception of the event, the precise gap is opened that calls for fidelity and the wager of truth. In an epoch that leaves less and less space for thinking, placing one's wager on the "semi-private room"[5] of the seminar may not be such a wayward idea, after all.

DIALOGICAL FIELDS

The term "dialogical fields" keeps appearing in the writing of various authors from the 1980s and the 1990s. It describes both a shared theoretical precept and a practice. To put it differently, the "orality" of the seminar should be understood as a specific amalgamation of a practice with its theoretical presuppositions (ultimately, the seminar produced a good deal of writing). Communication and dialogue became dominant theoretical preoccupations in the last decade of communism: Some of this material got published; some of it did not. A typical example would be Tzotcho Boiadjiev's article "The Dialogical Principle of Historic Cultural Research," which was distributed through the oral channels of the seminar and solicited so much discussion that the author wrote a response. Both texts treated the problem of communication methodologically; they both had an intense oral "career" in the context of seminar discussions; both were published—became publishable—after the fall of communism.[6]

Different currents contributed to this trend. The reception of Bakhtin—whose ideas of polyphony and dialogism were immediately seized upon as an oblique form of dissent from totalitarian monologism—was certainly a factor (in fact, two expat Bulgarians, Julia Kristeva and Tzvetan Todorov played a crucial role in Bakhtin's reception in France and elsewhere in the West). A less evident but more poignant incentive was the premature death of a major Bulgarian literary theoretician, Tzvetan Stoyanov. The posthumous publication of his mostly unfinished work coincided with the high times of the seminar. His writing, some of which took the form of dialogue and much of which dealt with the virtues of the spoken word, appeared accompanied by the commentary of his literary friends insisting that the truly great part of his thinking had taken place in *the voice* that articulated the thought. As Stoyanov himself put it in his essay "On Good Conversations," good conversations "are perhaps worth more than the hundreds of hours when we imagined we were doing something useful," for "the claim that good conversations are ephemeral does not correspond to the truth."[7]

The years during which Stoyanov's interpreters proclaimed him the master of conversation and the genius of the unwritten were also years of intense theoretical problematization of Plato's "unwritten doctrine." Very much in the spirit of the praise that Stoyanov received, it was emphasized that Plato's "dialectical communication" was thriving on the "element of speech." As Tzotcho Boiadjiev put it in his book *Plato's Unwritten Doctrine*,

> Plato's ideal is not mystical silence but the complete unfurling of the element of speech. . . . The most profound knowledge is not achieved through mystical illumination in solitude but through an intense cognitive effort, which is always carried out with the other.[8]

If both the reception of a contemporary figure and the interest in a classical figure focused on the act of enunciation per se, the Bakhtinian impact on these trends, sometimes discreet, sometimes overt, received a rather specific twist. The irreducible presence of the voice, of the *phonē,* in Bakhtin's ideas of polyphony and dialogism is conceptualized for and in writing. When it comes to the emphasis on the unwritten that surfaced in the 1980s discussions of Plato and Tzvetan Stoyanov and that, in fact, constituted a field far exceeding these two representative figures, the penchant was to render Bakhtin's ideas *literal*: Dialogue was no longer an internal aspect of the written word but the epitome of "good conversations."

Plato's *Symposium*, hence, was taken quite *à la lettre*, and so were other similar experiments such as the Florentine Platonic Academy. The seminar staged itself as a continuous polytopical banquet. There was a disregard for hierarchies; there was the view that knowledge is not taught but shared; there was the emphasis on the erotic-and-spiritual togetherness of people of the same mind: *circuitus spiritualis*. There was the explicit idea that this togetherness includes not only the present but also the past, not only the near, but also the distant. Derrida and Foucault, as totally inaccessible to us as Plato or Dante, were also as much a part of our living discussion. In a striking comment on Marsilio Ficino's school, Boiadjiev described this communicative telos in terms of the circle whose center is everywhere and whose circumference is nowhere. More soberly, Boiadjiev defined this trans-spatial and transtemporal communication as "drawing the dialogical projections of one's time in an unusual direction"[9]

What remains unwritten in this defense of the unwritten, whether written or spoken, is the tacit knowledge that censorship, which could still control publishing, no longer and perhaps never really controlled speaking, especially the speaking dialogically drawn in an "unusual direction." Among his "good conversations" Stoyanov places "the conversation of the oppressed and the tortured, above whom there weighs the shadow of a gloomy tyranny and for whom it would be dangerous to even dream together—and yet, there is hope in each syllable they utter."[10] The hope is that good conversations are, indeed, a material force, and if we do not always understand how and why things happened, it is because we do not know what people talked about.

Dialogue was hence valorized theoretically for the reason for which it was enacted. The result was that it returned to the cultural substratum where—its theoreticians were perfectly aware—it had its immediate support. But not unchanged. While, in the 1960s, the conversations for which Stoyanov was praised by those who remembered him were still informal and took place in selected cafes and private apartments, from the late 1970s on—which happened to be the time of the first publication of "On Good Conversations"—dialogism turned into an increasingly deliberate practice that disregarded the demarcation line between private and public in an effort to keep its distance from traditional practices and, simultaneously, to differentiate itself from the linguistic monopoly of the state. It found its proper medium for this effort in the academic setting and in *theory.*

THEORY AS THE DOME OF BEING

In the 1960s and the 1970s the situation with Bulgarian theory was rather peculiar. Condemned to isolation by the communist regime, the friends and university colleagues whom Tzvetan Todorov and Julia Kristeva left behind assumed a theoretical stance that might be described as vertical catastrophism: The impossibility for Bulgarian thinkers to participate in the "horizontal" international debates sought resolution in an attempt to assume a meta-position and integrate vertically the summa of theoretical thought tout court.[11]

Bulgarian theory was hence characterized by a sort of "domeness"—where the homonym of dome, the Bulgarian word *dom*, means precisely "home," thus sending us in the direction of Heidegger's famous statement about language: If language is the home of being then surely theory is its *dome.* The proper translation of dome in Bulgarian as *svod*, however, might refer, apart from the architectural structure, to the sky as firmament and to a library catalogue of catalogues. The dome-ness is for that matter a librarian's firmament, alias a heterogeneous congruence of authors, schools, disciplines, and a wide range of sciences, which goes far beyond any interdisciplinarity and whose receding horizons could be delineated only by the grand utopias of the totality of knowledge and languages. A circle whose center is everywhere. Kristeva's early work—but also Tzvetan Todorov's, viewed in this perspective—stands as the visible (French) articulation of this hidden agenda.

The agenda was, ultimately, to piece together the remnants of universalism and to confront the chiasm opened up between poststructuralist skepsis and structuralist epistemological optimism in a concerted effort to sustain the space for thinking. This is the ambition that the seminar, in its penchant for making things literal, took up in the 1980s with all its dialogical fervor. Concepts, schools, and disciplines proliferated, and they all had to meet in the "dialogical fields." Whether it worked as the utopia of total language or as Derridean enactment of difference, no one would be able to tell. Perhaps the utopia of the total language (Hermann Hesse's *Glass Bead Game* was a reference point, too) is what bred the differences. As Vladislav Todorov noted in a talk with my students, "We were using concepts like stones. We were flinging them at each other." Where concepts failed, performative acts were summoned: Wittgenstein's ladder, as already mentioned, was literally climbed and pushed down at a seminar presentation. Dialogue? Postmodern Moebius strip of reality and theory? This is what we *do*. In a manner, theory went wild. And yet, no matter how wild, theory it was. According to a popular anecdote of the time, the definition of "socialist realism"—the obligatory method, prescribed by the communist party—was "praising the authorities in a way they can understand." Seen in this perspective, the stratagem of the seminar was simplicity itself: It meticulously avoided praising the authorities in a way that completely dumbfounded them.

EXEMPLUM

As Tzotcho Boiadjiev put it, "A philosopher, with his conduct in life, becomes an 'example' (in the medieval sense of the word) and a 'personification' of his own theoretical intention: of his own teaching, embodied as an existential act." This requirement presupposes a "correspondence between words and deeds, between intellectual discernment and ethical integrity, between 'style of thinking' and 'style of living.'"[12]

Early leaking of Michel Foucault's lectures in Berkeley in 1983 and at the Collège de France in 1984 reformulated this issue in terms of parrhesia.[13] With the divisive poignancy of the political clashes immediately after the fall of the regime, Vaclav Havel was brought up as an "exemplum" simultaneously via Foucault and opposed to Foucault, as the paradigmatic "Eastern" versus the paradigmatic "Western" intellectual. Alexander Kiossev, the proponent of this view, defines Havel as "parrhesiast" in the sense that Foucault brought forth: as incorporating the rapport ("the harmonic relation") between truth and self, between "words" and "deeds," between "saying it all" and the biography of the person who says it. Kiossev draws a dramatic division between totalitarian and democratic societies in terms of the usages of truth that they impose. The parrhesiast is *the* type of intellectual that played a political role in opposing the communist regimes in Eastern Europe. Parrhesia makes sense in the face of tyranny but becomes a trap in the context of a democracy because it entails speaking about truth as a transcendent signified. Conversely, the critical questioning of truth and the exposure of its multiple workings as normalizing power is consistent with democracies but is too weak to resist totalitarian regimes.

This division between Eastern and Western intellectuals implies, therefore, a (self-critical) division between the head-on challenging of tyranny and the *différance* forms, which the seminar nourished. From this point of view the seminar was too "Western" at the improper time and in the improper place. In contrast to the sharp disparity between "Eastern" and "Western" intellectual experience that this division introduces, the second approach, which singles out Russian-Georgian philosopher Merab Mamardashvili as its example, tends to see continuity rather than fracture. In this second approach, the gesture of the political dissident is waived aside in favor of the concept of philosophical *inakomislie*, where *inakomislie* means literally "different thinking." Yet thinking itself in this usage has an aspect we might describe as parrhesiastic or, at the least, exemplary: as something like "living in difference," "living in/as thinking." "One cannot have philosophy without a philosophical form of life," Deyan Deyanov, the promoter of this view, told me.

In fact, one could argue that totalitarian regimes, based as they are on the premises of the one truth, are especially vulnerable to the proliferation of discourses (such is my claim drawn from the seminar experience), while contemporary democracy with its ease at multiplying spurious differences is in need precisely of parrhesia. The two positions thus seem to exclude each other and yet are linked in a manner that could be described, after Žižek, as a parallax gap: "the confrontation of two closely linked perspectives between which no neutral common ground is possible."[14] While neither is completely true, they both are necessary and require a structural synchronic functioning, which would reveal the truth in the irreducible gap between them, in the traumatic core that severs them and keeps them together.

HETEROTOPIAN HOMONYMY

It might sound like too much of an anecdote to declare Gorbachev to be an unwitting anti-Derridean. The fact nevertheless is that the two terms with which he deconstructed the Eastern bloc system—which he took over from Lotman, which fitted the ethos of the seminar with an uncanny seamlessness, and which might look like a negative of writing and deconstruction—were glasnost ("voice-ness") and perestroika ("reconstruction").

This book is not so much about the seminar per se but rather about such consternating turnarounds as the one surfacing in the encounter between "writing" and "glasnost." They foreground an inherent specular aspect of the Cold War division that caused mirror-like inversions of concepts to the two sides of the geopolitical confrontation. With a reference to Foucault's definition of heterotopia, to which I will return again and again in what follows, they can be described as heterotopian homonyms: conceptual doppelgängers that simultaneously represent, contest, and invert each other.

The redoubling of Hegel's fateful term *Aufhebung* as a raising up to the West of Germany and as a taking down to the revolutionary East offers an amusing and, at times, uncanny parable of this inversion. It involves a curious twist from apocalypse to sexual difference whose "parallactic" aspect is sharply brought into focus through the groundbreaking debate between Judith Butler and Joan Copjec.[15] The central tenet of humanism, "man," is another such story.[16] Toward the end of the communist regime, it appeared to be quite finished on the one side and quite as unfinished on the other side of the mirror.

When it went unrecognized—or, still worse, when it was recognized but dismissed as annoying triviality—heterotopian homonymy caused a lot of bewilderment in the first decade after the fall of communism. I treat this issue in some detail in Chapter 2. Here I would like to note that, although for me personally the drama of misunderstanding took place in a gender context (triggering my search for lost unicorns), nevertheless, the sphere of gender was the one sphere where a genuine East-West exchange took place. With her keen perception for the juncture of conceptual paradox and political confusion, Joan Scott offers, in a keynote speech that she read in September 2000 at the Fourth European Feminist Research Conference in Bologna, an astute analysis of the vigor of this exchange and a powerful deliberation of both its failure and success.[17]

The specular reflexivity uncovered in heterotopian homonymy involved the two-way traffic of the utopian fantasy, which is the true center of my interest throughout the book. The utopian fantasy was attached to the illusion that what it dreamed about existed over there, to the other side of the looking glass. With a view to Badiou's observation that what the postcommunist people wanted was nothing other than what already existed, taking into consideration the effects of the mirror would amount to saying: Yes, what they wanted was nothing other than what already existed. Only, it did not.

So, what is it that the revolution lost by winning? What is it that revolutions lose by winning? Or, as Wendy Brown has aptly put it, "What kind of lost object is this?"[18] By way of cutting these preliminary remarks short, I would like to make it quite clear that my search for lost unicorns is not a book of remembering. It is, rather, an attempt to draw the dialogical projections of our time in an unusual direction. There, hopefully, what is lost to remembering could be regained in a "utopian imaginary that has no certainty"[19] and does not need one.

CHAPTER ONE

The Seminar: *Mode d'emploi*: Impure Spaces in the Light of Late Totalitarianism

To Stefan Marinov
In memoriam

I am Sybil and I tell you with brutality:
When something's talked about for too long,
It usually turns into reality.
—Ivan Stanev, "Performance and Punishment"

THEORY AND TERROR

The seminar? In Bulgaria? In the 1980s? Who would care about this? Yet over and beyond the nostalgia that drives the survivors into incessant squabbling over the fossils of the seminar,[1] there is the major mystery that the seminar—from its restricted elitist inception in the late 1970s to its spilling over from the bursting university auditoriums into street action and clashes with the police in the spring and summer of 1989—was produced as the dominant trajectory of the crumbling of totalitarian power. Thus, if we cannot say that the seminar brought down the totalitarian regime—although what did? there is no definitive answer yet—we can say for sure that the regime in Bulgaria brought about the seminar as the one major symptom of its demise. The seminar makes us face the enigma of an indomitable political, economic, and military machine disintegrated by discourse: by "glasnost," or—to put Gorbachev's unwittingly lethal term literally—by "voicing," that is, by the reverberation of sound in space.[2]

Immediately I have to add that there was something very specific about this reverberation so that even when, at its most lyrical, the seminar decided to sing, the result was the opera *Wittgenstein,* with Bertrand Russell and Ludwig Wittgenstein singing along with the native apparatchik sociologist Iribadjakov (all of them impersonated by seminar participants) and the chorus of "atomic facts" chanting "where is the soup?" (The soup, as well as the freedom of speech, was never quite there.) The specificity, in short, of this deadly resonance, of this Jericho terror that brought the walls tumbling down, was that it was theoretical. The Bolshevik Revolution and its later East European editions were theory turned into terror. The glasnost extremism enacted the downfall of terror as theory. Through a curious move that reversed the actualization of theory into the terror of totalitarianism, the end of totalitarian terror took a theoretical turn.

What made it possible to bring about the demise of a regime by theory (if we assume that this is, indeed, what happened) was the very structuring of the regime as total discursive control. Discursive control secures the prerogative of a particular discourse to emanate reality. The surest way for a discourse to *be* reality is through enforcing itself as the only discourse there is. Through discursive control, the regime effected what it *said* to be equivalent to what *was*: The result was an ontological confusion where ideological statements took the form of factories and factories produced poems.[3]

This maneuver, however—the positing of a power as discursive monopoly—makes it very vulnerable to the proliferation of discourses. Hence, the status of intellectuals. Intellectuals were plentifully manufactured by the regime in order to, on the one hand, keep up its discursive monopoly through the constant maintenance of the master discourse. They were organized in paramilitary unions and were monitored closely by the secret police, with which they had to engage in discussions of neo-Hegelianism, for example. On the other hand, they had to exemplify the dangers of transgressing, if ever so little, the rules of the one language game that was allowed. The regime needed dissidents. The punishment of dissidents ensured the observance of the fundamental law: "Thou shalt speak as thou shalt speak."

Seen in this perspective, the seminar appears enmeshed in paradoxes because it inhabited the discursive machine it was trying to outwit—a predicament that is not a reason to deny its logic, that is, the logic of its illogicality, as demonstrated by Joan Scott's analysis of the paradoxes of French feminism trapped in the rights of man discourse.[4] The paradox with regard to the East European intellectuals was the following: The regime was bound to produce its subversion in order to sustain itself; the intellectuals were trying to subvert a power to which they owed their inflated subversive status. Ultimately, the seminar was possible because of the premises it shared with the regime it was undermining: belief in unassailable discursive power.

This statement raises questions about the relationship between language and power and about what has been described as the "collapsing of power into language [that] marked the invention of modern politics" and that opened, within democracies, the possibility for power to be "subverted by a linguistic act."[5] Was the vulnerability of communism to linguistic dissidence a consequence of its deviation from or of its closeness to the democratic collapsing of power into language? Would such vulnerability accompany any type of discursive monopoly, or did it betray the origins of communism as an aborted Enlightenment project? These questions seem to be especially pressing in the context of the continuing marginalization of theoretical thinking. Highlighting the fact that the discursive disintegration of communism happened from within and succeeded in being more or less peaceful (violence occurred in places where the regimes metamorphosed into other types of discursive monopoly, be it nationalist or religious), the role of the seminar in the breakdown of the Bulgarian communist regime foregrounds the question of the role that theory will or will not continue to play in a world that is no longer haunted by the specter of communism but that is besieged by other specters. Does theory have a role to play in the context of religious discursive monopolies? Can it withstand the opaque power of the image through which the media operate in the "society of the spectacle"? Can it have a say in the face of contemporary metamorphoses of global politics? These are large issues. In this first approach to the workings of the seminar I will try to limit my task by placing it in the perspective that marked most of the East/West feminist exchanges (and, frequently, confrontations) in the decade that followed the collapse of the iron curtain and that came to be designated as the "transition" to democracy. In this perspective, questions of discourse were mediated by questions of public/private space. I will address the seminar in and beyond the specific sense that "space" acquired through this debate.

In articulating all these neat questions and intentions, however, I do not want to raise overly high expectations. The seminar was a collective experience that has remained and probably will remain incommunicable, partially because of the brutal change in the overall political and discursive framework, partially because of the seminar's inherent and unavoidably paradoxical antidiscursive drive. Insofar as the seminar was trying to destroy the discursive machine that structured it, it had to, somewhat inevitably, constitute itself as a discursive kamikaze.

APPROACHING THE SEMINAR

"The seminar? Is it something about Lacan?"—I was frequently asked when trying to introduce my topic. Lacan was a reference point, indeed, and an especially important figure in arguments concerning the morality of "method" and/or "shamanism" when trying to win over your seminar audience. And yet, Lacan was only one of the many il/legitimate examples of the oral versus the written, examples that, with all due excuses in the direction of Derrida, ultimately took the seminar back to Plato and to his "unwritten doctrine."

In its recourse to orality, to speaking rather than writing, to critical questioning as a "form of life," to the philosophical dialogue as an embodied experience, to collective inquiry through the art or the Eros, or, as it was finally formulated, the ars erotica of conversation, the seminar was a spontaneous indigenous growth to a large extent motivated by a censorship that could still control publishing but no longer controlled speaking. As Angel Angelov put it, " 'Dialogue' was a humanitarian mind-set, normative and unattainable, that was cultivated in intellectual circles in the '80s against the complacent and monological institutionalized discourse of the state. This mind-set presupposed the self-discipline of listening to the other while simultaneously neutralizing the noise of your internal authority. I wouldn't say that we were very successful, and yet, to this very day, I can recognize the people who did not belong to the circles where dialogism was valued as a norm of behavior."[6]

From the late '70s on, this humanitarian "cultivation of dialogism" involved proliferating circles of people and events. The Sofia University Department of Philosophy was one of the centers and possibly the site of the seminar's beginning, but there were other centers and, with the years, more and more events were organized in the framework of more and more academic institutions in and outside of Sofia. So far as I know, only one of the early seminars, the "Salon" of Nikolai Vassilev (one of four Sofia university professors who were later fired), took place in a private apartment. Most of the seminars, even at the early stages, chose at first to invade the smaller university offices and auditoriums and then gradually to move on to the larger ones. The attraction of official spaces was, apart from the drive to get into the open, one of sheer size. One of the most bizarre examples I can recall was a seminar on mathematical logic that took place in 1988 in the largest auditorium of Sofia University, with five hundred people listening carefully to the most obscure subject matter. A year later, a poetry reading held in the same auditorium drew a huge crowd that was trying to break into the central university building, while mounted police were trying to stop it.

Although normally the seminars began in official buildings, the boundaries between the private and the public were blurred. When seminars took place in official buildings, they needed, and did get, official authorization. Yet much of what was going on could not fit into the temporal, spatial, and ideological limitations of institutions and expanded into private spaces. A paper or a number of papers would be presented—if it were a paper, indeed, since much of what went on was simply spoken. A discussion would follow that would naturally overflow into all-night talking, drinking, partying. There was a carnivalesque flavor to this aspect of the seminar. For example, the New Year's Eve of 1984 was celebrated as a rather wild "conference" on George Orwell with portraits of Karl Marx dressed as Santa Claus hanging on the walls. There was a halo of other activities: exhibitions in private apartments, poetry readings, opera and theater productions. Something that might be called "disciplinary transvestism" was part of this carnivalization: with young philosophy professors singing in the opera *Wittgenstein* or a mathematical logician organizing a hugely popular "exhibition" with his "visual art."

Some of the seminars took place within the regular curriculum but attracted growing audiences that needed neither grades nor credits. In most cases seminars had an extracurricular status of one sort or another. Some of the seminars were run by a single individual; most were loosely organized and collective; some were held once a year after careful planning and preparation; others would run for years on a monthly, weekly, or whatever regular or irregular basis. Some stuck to strict academic requirements and relied on the precise quotation, elegant reference, polite revision; others indulged in scandals and performative interventions (*vîzpalenie*—"inflammation"; *iztsepka*—"cutting up") and looked for their precedents in dada and surrealism. The early seminars were usually focused on a single problem or author (be it Plato, Husserl, or Wittgenstein). They were exclusive and strictly professional in the hope of—among other things—keeping out informers. The hope was vain as we very well knew, although the full scope of the terrible truth revealed itself much later, with the slow and selective making public of the secret services archives. At the time, acting *as if* there were no informers became the norm of the day: a discipline of reversing the well-grounded and prevalent paranoia. In any case, the situation quickly changed, and the change was marked by the broadening of both the thematic and the disciplinary framework of the seminars.

An easy way to describe this change, which gave rise to a recurrent image of the library and of polyglotism (with or without reference to Borges' "Babylonian Library"), is to describe it as cumulative: people came with their individual research agendas and were incorporated into the seminar. The hermeneutic principle of "listening to all the witnesses" was implemented in an uncompromising manner. The number of discourses that was thus accumulated was staggering and not very easy to place under the label of interdisciplinarity. There was a negative quality, an aspect of absence and emptiness, to this proliferation. It implied, in its totality, no schools, no authorities, no continuities, no allegiances, no demarcated "language game" communities. Inspired by the vision of the Total Book, this was a quest that knew the book would never be found. It roamed; it strayed. At the time, I called this straying, which strikes me today as a premonition of browsing, the "method of hovering among the bookshelves." Unaware that my "method" had a rather unique referent, that is, the seminar, I claimed that it was a faithful description of some general condition, namely, the "postmodern library." "In its finished form," I asserted, the aimless "straying" and "hovering" among the bookshelves takes the form of a capsule moving with the speed of light. In it, the postmodern reader has all the books in the universe and an eternity to read them.[7]

Yet, it was not as simple as that. Incommensurability was frequently discussed, yet everything was accepted as commensurable. On the one hand, no discourse was allowed to play the role of metadiscourse, but, on the other hand, no "differend" was allowed, no irreducible residue that could preclude further discussion. Getting together, not the lonely capsule, was the rule. Plato and Marsilio Ficino cast their long shadows. Neologisms sprang, delineating a sort of linguistic *comme il faut*. There was snobbery; there were inner circles; there were fights among the different circles along methodological, ideological, or other lines of contention; and there were power games as to who would be the star and who would be the "shaman." Through all this, the seminar had its ways of influencing the directions of individual endeavors. If it was felt at some point that a certain type of discourse was underrepresented, it could be commissioned as a sort of individual obligation to the group. This was how I was christened a feminist. I was asked to present feminism. I answered I could not do this with a clear conscience because I did not know enough. The answer was, "It doesn't matter. You *are* a feminist." So I made a presentation entitled "Feminism: Personification and Collage," in which I offered my physical presence as an exegesis of feminism. Ultimately, through its trust in a performative commensurability, the seminar posited itself as a unified field in which all actualized, possible, or, if need be, impossible discourses, whatever they were, were expected to operate as a concerted search.

This broadening was to a large extent intentional and accompanied by an effort to create a dialogue not simply among individuals but also across schools and disciplines. Some degree of self-reflexivity was probably inevitable. In an effort to ground itself in social reality and, more or less consciously, tap hidden reservoirs of resistance, the seminar placed the discussion of communication, power, and everyday life among its ongoing preoccupations.[8] Three wings were formed in the process. The "young Marxians" played an important role as a legitimizing buffer between the seminar and the regime. The "postmodernists" represented the poststructuralist and postmodern returns of "Eastern" formalism and structuralism that formed the traditional noncommunist theoretical background in Bulgarian academia.[9] The "classicists" or "medievalists" were united through their object rather than their method (which might vary from hermeneutics to semiotics and, more explicitly after the changes, to theology): They did, as a matter of fact, work on classical and medieval culture, which the regime could not really ban and yet did not particularly love. Beyond this, there were the mathematicians, the poets, the playwrights. In the fall of 1987, one last attempt was made to create a somewhat more rigorous frame for developments that were clearly becoming unmanageable: This is how the Synthesis seminar was created. It seems, however, that the seminar had already reached its limit.

In the early summer of 1988, the seminar "Power and Identity" was having one of its sessions in the Faculty of Slavic Studies when we heard disturbing noises from outside and moved to another auditorium. Using the opportunity of a cultural event in the courtyard of the university, the poet Peter Manolov had driven the rain-soaked crowds into a complete frenzy with a long poem consisting mostly of obscene abuse addressed to the party and government leaders. The end was coming. A year later[10] the seminar was transformed and, in fact, dissolved into a political movement proper under the umbrella of *Ecoglasnost*, a small ecological club, which by 1990 had acquired a membership of 120,000 and played an important role in the political events of the '90s.

PARRHESIA AND *INAKOMISLIE*

There is no doubt that the momentum for the seminar was political: If nothing else, its dramatic and immediate disintegration after the changes demonstrates this. However, the questions remain open as to the relationship between the seminar's highly theoretical, interdisciplinary functioning, on the one hand, and its actual role in the ensuing political events, on the other. How did belated modernists, postmodernists, feminists, Frankfurtians, young Marxians, Heideggerians, neo-Kantians, classicists, and hermeneutic, Christian Orthodox, and Catholic scholars talk to each other? What discursive ingredient made the continuous cohabitation of such a wild variety of disciplines and methods possible? If bringing down the regime—a possibility never discussed that bluntly and until the last not quite believed in—was the unsaid that kept the dialogue going, does this mean that the seminar did in fact influence the bringing down of the regime? What mysterious force drove the rebellious crowds toward the *university building* as the locus from which freedom was expected to emerge?

In subsequent years, key seminar figures have suggested two conceptual frameworks for addressing these questions. The first is Alexander Kiossev's. Kiossev reconsiders Vaclav Havel, simultaneously via Foucault and opposed to Foucault, as the paradigmatic "Eastern" versus the paradigmatic "Western" intellectual.[11] Kiossev regards Havel, who himself opposed the term "dissident," as "parrhesiast" in the sense that Foucault brought forth in his 1983 lectures at Berkeley and in his 1984 lectures at the Collège de France.[12] *Parrhesia*, a Greek term, is highlighted by Foucault as a specific usage of truth that relies on what might be described as the "incorporation" of truth. The parrhesiastic game involves the rapport ("the harmonic relation") between truth and self, between "words" and "deeds," between "saying it all" and the biography of the person who says it. The persuasiveness of such truth—a truth of the type "the king is naked" that demands courage in the face of tyranny—does not belong to the order of discourse and does not draw its power from argument. Parrhesia is, in fact, frequently opposed to rhetoric and the rhetorical techniques of persuasion. The persuasiveness of parrhesia comes rather from "a kind of ontological harmony" between what one says and what one is, between *logos* and *bios*. It speaks of a truth that one guarantees with one's body and one's life. Havel's famous demand for "living within the truth,"[13] with all the ensuing risks that this demand cost him, is revealed, according to Kiossev, as a parrhesiastic act par excellence.

Foucault's problematization of parrhesia, unfinished as it is, follows the shifts of meaning that it underwent from Euripides to Epictetus, emphasizing that throughout these shifts the Cartesian severance between what one believes to be true and what *is* true did not occur. Hence parrhesia, in this "naive" Greek sense, according to Foucault, can no longer occur in the modern epistemological framework. In his analysis, Kiossev, who is concerned with the post-totalitarian 1990s, underscores precisely the risks of a return to presumptions that close off the division between "I say as I am" and "what I say is the truth." The problem, he believes, is that, while parrhesia had a role to play in the face of totalitarian regimes, its usage in the context of new democracies leads to fundamentalist concepts of truth. Kiossev's Foucault/Havel juxtaposition is thus framed by two important presuppositions: that parrhesia has no place and is in fact dangerous in democratic societies because it involves a slippage from the correspondence between logos and bios to the claim for the possession of truth per se and that, in contrast, the parrhesiast is *the* type of intellectual who played a political role in opposing the communist regimes in Eastern Europe. The rest of us "were playing," Kiossev told me in conversation. In his early text on the Synthesis seminar he envisions that the seminar generation would have been assimilated into the official communist structures of power.[14]

Kiossev seems, therefore, to draw a dramatic division between totalitarian and democratic societies in terms of the usages of truth that they impose. Against the grain of Foucault's own conceptualization of parrhesia as "care of the self," Kiossev is distrustful of "living in," of "incorporation," and of "I say as I am."

In contrast to this distrust and to the sharp disparity between "Eastern" and "Western" intellectual experience that it introduces, the second approach tends to see continuity rather than fracture. In this second approach, the gesture of the political dissident—"living within the truth"—is waived aside in favor of thinking through the concept of philosophical *ina-*

komislie, where *inakomislie* means literally "different thinking." Yet thinking itself in this usage has an aspect we might describe as parrhesiastic—as something like "living in difference," "living in/as thinking." As Foucault's cryptic remark from the Collège de France notes has it, "Shouldn't the true life be a life radically other?"

Socrates might be as important an emblem for this view as it was for Foucault's development of the figure of the parrhesiast—the Socrates for whom "thinking meant living. The animate word, the living word, the word that spreads on the occasion of and at the moment of meeting the other." This description of Socrates by Jean-Pierre Vernant is, in fact, his description of the Georgian-Russian philosopher Merab Mamardashvili who, like Socrates, "was not a man of the written word."[15] The fact that Mamardashvili *wrote* and that he reached the seminar in the 1980s in the form of smuggled manuscripts did not have an effect on this belief in a constitutive orality that harmonized—a point to whose shifting status I will keep returning—with the seminar's obsession with the voice and the *phonē.* As Deyanov initially put it (he later changed his position), Mamardashvili is a difficult thinker because of "the layering of heterogeneous philosophemes . . . but also because of the oral form of his philosophizing, inseparable from his philosophical style. Not a spoken philosophy that could be written down but a spoken philosophy as opposed to the written one."[16]

For Deyanov, it is important to emphasize that philosophical "thinking differently" survives the political exigencies that have mobilized it. "We all shared the belief in the need for a critique of modernity," he told me apropos the seminar. "Beyond the critique of the status quo, we always envisioned the critique of modernity." Deyanov's bringing forth of Mamardashvili as the emblematic East European intellectual from the last decades of the regime is carried out as part of this sustained critique. Once again, Foucault is evoked side by side with "Eastern" theory. Deyanov, however, reads Foucault via Mamardashvili's "nonclassical rationality"[17] and, conversely, Mamardashvili via

Foucault, in order, ultimately, to demonstrate the potential of philosophical *inakomislie* to counter normalization by creating "dialogic fields . . . where different interpretational strategies, genres, and individual styles can meet. We insist on this because we believe that the thinking polyphony that opens dialogic fields for both the provocative explorations and the voices that counter them, is the condition that makes a new critical publicity possible."[18]

AN ASIDE WITH SOME QUESTIONS

I believe that a split between political and philosophical dissidence as exemplified in the contrasting figures of Havel and Mamardashvili will not serve to illuminate either the seminar or the circumstances that turned it into the symptom of—or, possibly, the illustration of—what brought about the regime's demise. Yet there is a mysterious point of convergence between Kiossev's and Deyanov's accounts that I have, with some approximation, referred to as "incorporation." Did "incorporation" "matter" (with reference to Judith Butler's pun)? If incorporation did, indeed, matter, which type of it—the incorporation of "living within the truth" or the incorporation of "living in/as thinking differently"—could and perhaps did matter more?

At this point what "matters" in the convergence of the figures of Havel and Mamardashvili is the displacement of the term "dissident," a displacement exemplified by Havel's own resistance to this name. A "dissident" was the product of (external, Western) media. "He was not a dissident," said a former colleague of Stefan Marinov, the man to whom this chapter is dedicated. "He simply wanted to say what he thought." A person who "simply wanted to say what s/he thought" and did not reach the Western media as "dissident" would, during communism, become a mental clinic patient, a prisoner, the victim of a car accident. By avoiding the term "dissident" and speaking in terms of parrhesia and *inakomislie*, of bios/logos harmony, and of embodied thinking differently, I will attempt—with all the risks that such an attempt entails—to look into ways systems structured as total discursive control might be challenged from within. In this effort, my discussion of the seminar will, for the time being, waive aside so far as possible the role that the West as the "outside" played in bringing about the fall of communism, including the role of an intellectual (as opposed to consumerist) utopia born of our isolation.

The utopia was nevertheless there (I will address it in the second chapter) and the outside was also there, and interested. There are discursive systems without an outside: the system of sexual difference, for example, or the system of a presumable globalized cyberspace world. My attempt to isolate the workings of the seminar from the various transactions with the outside is, from that point of view, an oblique attempt to approach the possible forms of resistance to such systems. The contemporaneous Western theories that the seminar plentifully referred to will hence be regarded as a steady drizzle of meteorites from outer space that sometimes burned while still in the stratosphere, sometimes reached the seminar ground in a more or less smelted form.

SPACES AND SEMI-SPACES

In and outside the context of the seminar, it has been argued that communism failed because it did not succeed in completely annihilating the private sphere as it intended to do.[19] After the changes, one of the continuations of this argument could be found in the East/West debate about feminism, or rather, about the Eastern resistance to feminism.[20] This debate centered on a discussion of the public/private distinction (displacing, in most cases, the Habermasian terms that were supposed to provide its background), with Westerners frequently assailing and Easterners frequently defending the political importance that the private space acquired during the totalitarian regime. In the latter case, the family was conceptualized as a reserve of alternatives to the repressive political apparatus.

According to this argument, the family was that private area where people could find refuge from the control of the state, and as such it was the locus of solidarity, rather than confrontation, of the sexes in their common resistance to the alienating political structure.[21] As one commentator characteristically put it: "Political discussions were conducted around the kitchen table; the home represented the only place for open discussion like this; it was here rather than in any public sphere that the possibility for transcendence occurred."[22]

This optimistic position, which was, perhaps, meant to demonstrate the readiness of the Central European middle-class family for European structures, ignored the somewhat more complicated history of gender manipulation that the different communist regimes implemented.[23] With this history taken into account, it has been argued that, on the contrary, the duplicity resulting from a private life that was cynically distanced from the totalitarian public sphere in fact sustained the regime.[24] The family, with its sacrosanct private life, was part of the duplicity. Further, it could be argued that at least in some of the countries the traditional structures of the family reproduced the conditions that made society as a whole susceptible to the charms of fundamentalist and totalitarian attitudes, be they communist, fascist, nationalist, and so on.

Still other accounts insist on the impossibility of reducing the problem of the sustainability of communism to the private/public dichotomy. The public space, to begin with, was not really public: It was an "as if" publicity and an "as if" space that has been described as "theatrical" or "make believe:"[25] as spurious, ritualized, and flat. This quasi public space of never-ending buffoonery could be approached through the distinction between understanding political space in "Newtonian terms," as a mere container, a void in which commensurable and autonomous agents move, and in "Einsteinian terms," where actors "constitute, as they are constituted by" a specific political space.[26] Viewed in an "Einsteinian" perspective, the "as if" public space of "negative but equal citizenship"[27] that characterized the space of communism would appear as the product of a specific bifurcation of the political "gravitational field." This spurious space would be constituted by "negative citizens" that exert no gravity and have no mass or weight of their own. These citizens of spurious publicity would be equal in their weightlessness. Their commensurability would be the commensurability of shadows. As phantoms, they would partake of the equality in the land of the dead. They would be like the "dreams of a corpse."[28] Their space would not simply be absolute in the terms of Newton and Einstein. It would be the space of Elysium.

And yet, there was the presumable locus where real discussion, real decisions, and real power were exercised: the dreaming corpse itself, the "mummacrum of power."[29] Behind the gravitationless space of phony publicity there was the "black hole" of utter opaqueness and absolute gravity. Havel described this still center of omnipresent control (the hidden source of discursive monopoly) as the place where "the center of power [was imposed as] identical with the center of truth."[30] The inscrutable folding in upon itself of this invisible space might be termed conspiratorial, and its genealogy might very well take us to the history of Russian terrorism and, beyond it, to the specific manipulation of representation that terrorism involves.[31] Suffice it to say at this point that what appeared as public space was the façade of a "privatization" of political representation by the party headquarters and involved a conspiratorial bifurcation of the "privatized" public domain into, on the one hand, the weightless, theatrical spuriousness and, on the other, the invisible black star emitting the ghostly show.

If the quasi publicity of communism presented such convolutions of space, it is hardly surprising that the so-called private space to which commentators tend to attribute the dual function of subverting and containing communism was no less ambiguous.[32] Whatever this formation was to begin with, it did not stay put but grew into a sort of silent duplicate of the public-cum-conspiratorial space. The economic aspects of this shadowy area have been referred to as the "gray network." Beyond economy and the exigencies of overcoming deficits, however, there lay the further capacity of this quasi private space to veritably duplicate both the "make-believe" and the conspiratorial roles, relations, and hierarchies with its own. Deficits would be overcome through "buddies"; dissidents would be saved by "uncles"; "aunties" who happened to operate one of the scanty state-controlled copy machines would keep samizdat going. Because of its reduplicating power this pervasive formation was called the "second network."[33] At its last stages, the regime was acutely aware of the danger and tried to counter it by identifying it as the "little truth" and opposing it to the great communist truth. The fear was well grounded because, unlike parrhesia, the "little truth" (which ultimately was the truth of survival) was silent, cautious, cunning, and ubiquitous. The second network offered no discourse; it was indifferent to discursive resistance.[34] This made it, in sharp contrast to parrhesia, practically immune to a persecution obsessed with discursive control.

The seminar might be seen as owing the very possibility of its existence to this particular failure of the system. Ensuring through the Dubcek-Gorbachev fallacy a sort of buffer in the conspiratorial structures (i.e., there were apparatchiks that supported the seminar because they wrongly believed the regime could coexist with freedom of speech), the seminar created its own network and thus struggled to create its own space. Dimitrina Petrova (a philosopher, one of the founders of *Ecoglasnost*) rightly noted in conversation with me that we had come to a point where having a prestigious standing in the seminar was widely considered more important than having an official career. The seminar disregarded not only the party hierarchies that were deemed more and more unacceptable but also the academic ones: Some of the participants had academic positions; others did not; selected students took part in the seminar on an equal basis, and so forth. Key figures who ensured the seminar's functioning through their connections in the conspiratorial space were treated with open hostility and disdain, and yet they continued to attend the seminar and to take part in its discussions so that the very hostility they had to counter was articulated as part of the ongoing debates. Should one immigrate? Should one go underground? Should one make a party career and change things from within? The seminar opposed all these traditional options for Eastern intellectuals and insisted on opening its own "impure" space. Parrhesiasts appeared and flourished in this new environment. And yet, parrhesia as exemplified by Havel was only one of the discursive games that the seminar nourished. Before I look into the topological operations that accompanied these games, one further aspect of communist space deserves to be mentioned.

EROTIZATION: THE THIRD SEX

What most accounts of space during communism omit, I believe, is the mystery of erotization. As a much more logical discursive machine than the French bourgeois revolution, communism resolved the paradox created for women by the "rights of man" discourse by giving women rights (spurious and theatrical as they were) insofar as they were men. There could be no "woman question" and no feminism if women were to have rights. In order to have rights, women had to not exist. More precisely, they had to be preserved only as a moment in an ever-increasing maleness according to the formula

Men → Women → Men'

Unlike Claude Lévi-Strauss's account of the exchange of women, in this account it is both men and women who take part in the circulation of exchange, where men, by analogy with Marx's formula of capitalism

Money → Commodity → Money',

take the place of the forever increasing capital and women are the commodity that mediates this increase.[35] This is the *differentia specifica* of the new world of communism: instead of capital, it produces the new man, Man'. Man' is, in fact, a new, third sex that has reappropriated his rib[36] and whose genitals are symbolically represented by the intertwining of the hammer and the sickle.[37] Man' is hence a self-sufficient creation that sustains itself in a "a sort of intertwined, ejaculating but somehow permanent erection" best exemplified by Vera Mukhina's famous sculpture of the worker and the peasant whose proud upright bodies entangle above their heads a hammer and a sickle.[38]

The creation of Man' was dictated by a project to do away with sexuality altogether. As Andrei Platonov characteristically put it, "Having found the Good in the sexual feeling, people were petrified."[39] To combat this general petrification, communist regimes at their inception were very repressive of sex; youthful folly was not tolerated, and adultery was punished through workers' collectives, frequently resulting in the blocking of professional and party careers. The trajectory that led from this repressiveness to the sexual laissez-faire of the later decades of communism still needs to be elucidated. I am not sure about the extent to which this trajectory was specific to Bulgaria. Aware as it was that the country had produced no serious challenges to the regime in the way Hungary, Czechoslovakia, and Poland had, the seminar offered an ironic view of the consecutive outbursts of sexual excess as the specific Bulgarian response to the dramatic political events in the other countries of the region.[40]

Whatever the reason, there was a conspicuous overall tendency toward sexual liberalization. Moreover, it is clear that the workplace was the locus of the loosening of morals. In general, the workplace became a huge and blurry border between the various spaces already mentioned. It was heavily infiltrated with conspiratorial monitoring and, at the same time, it sheltered a most amazing display of the pompous spuriousness of the public space in that it was expected to produce the working class as the "leading metaphor of party ideology" rather than goods. Yet, it was also a place continuously and systematically "appropriated" by the "gray" networks, which corrected, so far as possible, the deficits typical of the regime. The coded erotization participated in the privatization that positioned the workplace midway between work and leisure.[41] The workplace thus became the locus of consumption and sexualization. Notoriously, during communism one went to work in order to chat, flirt, hear the latest political jokes, and do one's shopping through the gray networks.

Work also occupied a hybrid position with respect to the conceptualization of gender. While the conspiratorial structures were almost entirely dominated by the male phratry, while the private sphere of the family was allowed to stick to its traditional patriarchal roles, work was the place where women were comparatively free from both the state and the family patriarchies. This was a mute tendency, however, that lacked any clear articulation. Thus, while the private sphere had its age-old articulation of roles (boys will be boys), while the male conspiratorial structure emitted its make-believe third sex messages (we are all equal because we are all Men'), the workplace, as the only place where practical redefinitions of gender happened, was never—given the communist ban on any serious discussion—provided with a language for its gendered aspects. It operated through an indiscriminate mixture of the traditional and the official discourses and, since it was not easy to reconcile them, resolved the conflict in a sort of carnivalesque way. This multiple layering can be exemplified through the manner in which March 8 was celebrated: The state offered its repetitive tedious speeches on the equality it had granted to women in making them as good as men; husbands and lovers spent the day in endless lines to buy flowers (for even in cases like this the deficit was insurmountable); and workplaces, with or without the men in them, booked all restaurants or, even better, used their offices to organize veritable spring orgies in honor of the "day of the female colleague."

No matter how specific, the seminar was a workplace. It thus shared—and expanded—the hybridity that characterized the communist workplace. As already mentioned, the seminar indiscriminately occurred in institutional buildings with the consent of official authorities and then spilled over into private apartments that became the site of discussions, expositions, and theater and opera performances. Sometimes all this seemed to be part of the educational system; sometimes it looked like a perennial party. Because the idea of working or office hours was lost in the process, the seminar amounted to round-the-clock cohabitation. The most brutal comment on this relentless eroticized togetherness is, perhaps, Ivaylo Ditchev's image of the Siamese twins joined forehead to forehead in a sort of perennial and inexorable cerebral copulation.[42]

The "promiscuous closeness" of the seminar functioned nevertheless as a verbal "exhausting of the drive" (both phrases are Vladislav Todorov's). Volumes of commentaries were produced on Plato's *Symposium*, on Marsilio Ficino, on eroticism throughout the ages and in any imaginable context. The philosophical Eros. The Eros of antiquity. The erotic world of the medieval person. An essay on the erotization of ethics. The ars erotica of conversation. Of reading. Of everyday existence. The erotic and communication. Rhetoric and the erotic. The Eros of communism. As a "knight of the prosthesis," Eros was an Eros of discourse—"Eros is what happens in the dialogue"—and an Eros of distance, after all.[43] The verbal handling of the erotic gave rise, in its turn, to a series of essays on "writing and seduction" where (predominantly female) authors brought into focus a selected company of literary seducers notorious for their fear of sex.[44] A pun on Wittgenstein's famous ending of *The Tractatus Logico-Philosophicus*—"Whereof one cannot speak, thereof one must quote"[45]—turned the (men's) lips into "quotation marks" and provided an ironic summing up of the seminar's oral eroticism.

Hence, the seminar both shared and articulated, with various shades between sublimity and parody, the erotization that characterized the workplace. The result was that academic structures and, more important, the function that the regime ascribed to intellectuals were "privatized," and private life (whatever private life meant during communism: sex, the family, friendship) was expropriated and all but erased. In practice, the seminar left no time for private life and assimilated it into its perpetual activities. Friendships, coupling, and everyday concerns swam in this soup as little pieces of unstable vermicelli. An odd state of affairs, to be sure. And yet, a certain type of hybridization (if hybridization is sufficient to denote this impure nexus) could be both unavoidable and constitutive of some specific places that have to allow for the appearance of the unfamiliar, the different, and the unforeseen. Before being anything else, Eros is the *daimon* of the "impure," of the productive in-between.

AN ASIDE WITH SOME FIGURES

One of the major postcommunist splits in the communal and communicative ethos of the seminar occurred when in 1992 one of the young participants, Amelia Licheva, pointed out that the post-totalitarian accounts of the seminar systematically erased the participation of women.[46] The response that she received was, generally, that it was so because . . . it was so. Since it is highly unlikely that someone will go seriously into the trouble of reconstructing (if this is at all possible) who attended seminars and how often, who spoke and how often, I decided to attempt to create some statistics based on the collections that, after the changes, were published from the seminar proceedings.

The participating women turned out to be around 30 percent. After the changes, there was an attempt to revive the glorious past with a weekly seminar on "media and myths." Two collections came out of it with women's participation dropping to 4–5 percent.

All sorts of reasons have probably combined to yield such results.[47] At this point I would like to single out one of them. After the changes, women from East European academia came under considerable pressure—both ideological and economical, for there was the question of sheer survival—to drop the dusty books and turn to the green tree of life, that is, violence against women, sexual abuse, and sexual harassment. The pressure of imposed priorities tended to treat East European women as empirical objects of anthropological inquiry and should be recognized as one of the (more or less) silent components of the East European resistance to feminism: with feminism being for the most part wrongly perceived as a monolithic doctrine of one sort or another rather than as a field of contention that cuts across any problem and debate. In the decades that followed, the scene insofar as gender is concerned has changed beyond recognition. It even affected the Bulgarian language where, countering conscious feminist tendencies in other languages where nouns possess grammatical gender, the female grammatical gender so far as the professions are concerned has more or less disappeared. From hairdressers to members of parliament, Bulgarian women today use the male gender for themselves and for other women. The logic for this linguistic change is probably that, if femininity is to be perceived as by definition harassed, abused, and violated, then it should be preserved for prostitutes and models. Everybody else is a man. Curiously enough, Man' was finally realized after the demise of the communist project. Peggy Watson is justified in noting that the masculinization of post-totalitarian societies had a logic of its own, but that logic was also enhanced through structures imported, as Joan Scott points out, by external factors.[48]

ELYSIUM OR ABSOLUTE SPACE

The man to whom my paper is dedicated was a parrhesiast. He went through all the hell of communist persecution (the interrogations, the mental clinic, the confiscation of his property, the harassment of his family after he left) because of (among other things) a protest letter he wrote in the late sixties to Todor Zhivkov, the Bulgarian government and party leader for over thirty years. With the help of the "second network" and the international attention he succeeded in attracting, Marinov was eventually allowed to leave the country. His quarrel with communism, spectacular, ingenious, and full of mischievous invention as it was, came nevertheless accompanied by a *theory*: a theory of fundamental physics, as it happened to be. Stefan Marinov was a physicist who believed that Einstein was wrong. He was convinced that the speed of light was not the ultimate possible speed; that space was absolute and hence not curved by the mass of bodies; and that perpetual motion was conceivable and could be implemented.

After leaving the country, Marinov became an active participant in clandestine anti-Einstein movements. He came to visit Bulgaria in the summer of 1997, at a time when changes were apparently becoming irreversible. After the visit he attended an international conference in Greece related to his scientific preoccupations. On returning to Graz in Austria where he had been living on welfare for many years, he wrote three lucid farewell letters explaining that he had lost hope he would live to see Einstein refuted, and jumped to his death from the roof of the local library.

This death was Marinov's last demonstration of his uncanny parrhesiastic gift for leaving no space between thinking, speaking, and doing. Through it, Marinov offered a reading of the concurrence of his political and scientific defiance. If the fall of communism rendered Marinov's scientific agenda meaningless, it turns out that his theory of space was his form of resistance to communism. His subversive stance took on a theoretical cast. Through physics, Marinov was positing a topology of antitotalitarian subversion. With the space of communism collapsing, his theory of space lost sense—or at least, so it seemed to him.

Through this parable, all too neat perhaps, I am trying to bring into focus my belief that it is not that easy to sort out parrhesia from thinking differently, Havel from Mamardashvili. In the perspective of the seminar, Marinov's absolute space—the space that might give room to weightless citizens and a perpetuum mobile to resistance—discloses a certain necessity. The seminar would not exist without something that might be described as the ear of the absolute. A sort of librarian's or virtual Elysium, the seminar enacted the shadowy space of the dead. Walking through asphodel fields, it was absorbed in perennial discussions that would draw along anyone from Plato and Gaspara Stampa to Derrida. That the former were dead and the latter still living made no difference to the attentive cosmic ear in which the shadowy whispering finally coalesced. Like Dante in his dealings with the nether world, the seminar felt no duty to distinguish between the living and the dead. It perceived its utterances as disembodied voices communicable through a vibrating medium that presented no obstacle. Its ethereal universe suspected no hierarchies, borders, or compartmentalized zones. It was a world of thorough transmittability. We could overhear anything and imagined ourselves overheard (in an unwitting positivization of paranoia) from any given point in the continuum. The seminar was a perpetuum mobile of entwined, spiraling voices that, having once reverberated, would resound forever. It was a panphonia that would never fade away but only get richer and fuller. And while linguistic and translation problems were debated in the minutest possible details, the idea of language never disturbed our conviction that, in writing and speaking Bulgarian, we inhabited the same dimension as the texts that we read (in whatever language) and passionately referred to. The seminar positioned itself under an absolute decoding machine that would allow no sign to remain unseen, unheard, and unread in the horizon of eternity.

Yuri M. Lotman, the legendary semiotician from Tartu, provided us with an elaborate structure of this ultimate cosmic decoder, this apex where the multitudinous discursive witnesses attain their final hearing. Within and beyond the punctilious exploration of various sign systems, Lotman's work on what he defined as "semiosphere" is obsessed with the indestructibility of meaning. Meaning may be hidden, it may undergo changes and transformations (and we should study how they happen); it may get condensed and get rarified; it may acquire or lose dimensions through its interweaving with other meanings. Yet it never really disappears. Nonsense, noise, uproar, amnesia, the perfect eraser, or sheer stupidity (for it does exist, after all) are of the order of illusion. Networks over networks of meaning intersect in an infinite horizon of actual or potential readers. Sooner or later, here or elsewhere, they will be read. Nothing will be forgotten. No one will be forgotten. It will all vibrate on atomic, subatomic, stellar, and nebular levels. It is built into the elements. Even dead, it will survive the monody of your one-tone message, and, encoded, it will gush into the all-comprehending machine.

A NOTE ON THE LEAP FROM THE LIBRARY

The above description could serve as a description of the library or, alternatively, of cyberspace. The library, with or without reference to Borges, was one of the recurring themes of the seminar. That Marinov chose to kill himself by leaping from the roof of the library is a message I will choose to leave without comment here.

OBZHIVYAVANE

Incorporation—the term through which I tried to designate the mysterious overlapping of Havel and Mamardashvili in what Foucault's discussion of parrhesia has unraveled as an "ontological harmony" between logos and bios—is an imperfect and rather misleading translation of one of the many neologisms of the seminar. This neologism, *obzhivyavane*, comes from the Bulgarian word for "live" and might be rendered as something like "to surround with life by being surrounded with the life of" or "to make something (a concept, a theory, a situation, a place, or whatever) part of my life, assimilate it, and introject it into my life by infiltrating it with and penetrating it with my life; to take part in the life of something by letting it take part in my life; to live in by letting be lived in." The root for life should not be taken too dramatically, however. The word does not imply some irrational overwhelming life force. Neither should the prefix meaning something like "around" and "about" be taken too extremely. In regular cases when this prefix appears, it usually adds the idea of a certain gliding motion that covers and traverses the space that the motion concerns, without implying, however, the complete siege or capture of this space.

In fact, this neologism for "living about and around" was almost interchangeable with another neologism, *obgovaryam*, which attached the same prefix to the word for "speak." You surround something with your speaking, you speak around and about it, you gently embrace it on all sides with your words, and it thus becomes a part of your speech. Unlike other seminar neologisms that tended to emphasize extreme and excessive states and actions ("inflammation," "abscess," "cutting up," "engulfing," etc.), the living around and the speaking about have a quiet aspect that suggests a touch, a gliding skin-to-skin, and a tender, although also thorough, movement from the unfamiliar to the familiar, and from the distant toward the close. From that point of view, these terms might be regarded as antonyms of defamiliarization, of *ostranenie.* Could a combination between "lure" and "embrace"—not too tough and not too rough—indicate this movement? You enter a new house, and you lure it into your existence by embracing it with your life and with your speech. You hear a new word, and you lure it into your thinking by embracing it with your life and with your speech. You go to a foreign country, and you lure it into your biography by embracing it with your life and with your speech. In all this, it is the strange that is being drawn closer; it is the unfamiliar that is being gently charmed in. Living as luring and speaking as embracing are hence inherently impure; they are the impurity of space per se.

The origin of these words turned out to be untraceable. Some thought they invented them. Others thought they might be coming from terms in Alfred Schutz and his concerns with everyday life.[49] Still others believed they might be existentialist terms of one sort or another, maybe from Heidegger. No one was sure of the definitions, and the suggestion was to go back to their uses in whatever seminar texts had been preserved. Vladislav Todorov, to whom I have frequently referred and who was the author of a great number of the seminar neologisms, thought there was no point in trying to track down the origin or, indeed, the meaning of these words. "The words that we were using then," he wrote to me, "had an erotic rather than a conceptual function; they were an object of desire rather than of knowledge; their value lay in pronouncing them and even ceremoniously shouting them, so that they caused somatic rather than semantic vibrations, something like inhabiting a secret collective sonorous *ontos*."

Todorov's injunction not to look for the meaning of the words I was asking for comes, in fact, very close to what I believe the words mean. It evokes a cohabitation and a lived togetherness through the agency of the somatic and erotic reverberations of speaking. The indestructibility of meaning, of the meaning that is read by the absolute ear and that, via the wide arc of the political, the erotic, and the quasi religious, enables the "thinking polyphony," turns out to be, in Todorov's description, an effect of reverberation. So are we back to the enigma of the *phonē*, of Bakhtin's polyphony not so much in the terms of some general dialogism but in terms of his idea of the "internal" proliferation of the "word" through the inscrutable agency of the "voice"? Bakhtin's "word" is an irreducible twist of reverberating multiplicity. Polyphony was his theory of the hope that the monological word of the master discourse will never be able to withstand the infraction of the *phonē*, of the indestructible explosive potential of voicing. Recalling that Gorbachev's terms that proved so lethal to the system were *glasnost*, a term that echoes Bakhtin and plays a crucial role in Lotman's discussion of nineteenth-century political unrest in Russia, and *perestroika*, a term which is also derived from Lotman, one might make a strong case in favor of the theoretical *obzhivyavane*, the embrace, that is, of living and thinking in the *phonē*.

Obzhivyavane would thus name the luring of the unfamiliar and the new into the reverberating borders of multiple dialogic voices. I will stop short of this optimistic conclusion, however, in order to take heed of some further sounds and echoes.

KNOCK, KNOCK, KNOCK

One of the weirdest of the many weird texts that the seminar produced was Ivan Stanev's "farce," "Performance and Punishment," which provided a rather dark and caustic comment on the seminar's preoccupations. The farce is written in the form of Old Greek tragedy, or rather, cantata, for we are back to the very beginnings of drama here, with just a chorus and its leader on stage, a fitting dramaturgical description of the seminar situation. This hybrid between Samuel Beckett and Aeschylus stages (or at least claims to be doing this) a paradigmatic nineteenth-century novel about agency, presenting the totalitarian metamorphosis of the utmost transgressive act: While in Dostoyevsky's novel *Crime and Punishment* murder is the crime, in Stanev's farce it is an obscene violation of language that verges on the imbecile.

In Dostoyevsky's novel, the protagonist Raskolnikov commits a senseless murder in order to prove his exceptionality and become Napoleon; he does not become Napoleon but is reborn as a moral individual, a "new man." *Crime and Punishment* is a classical rendition of the well-justified Russian anxieties concerning the road from theory to violence, following as it does the metamorphosis of "Western history" into "Eastern theory" and, beyond it, to terror. A later modernist reworking of this Russian obsession takes the murderer not to moral salvation but to the madhouse: Leonid Andreev's protagonist of "The Thought" has eventually to realize that he does not know whether he murdered to prove the impeccable power of his logic or whether his logic was the cunning of the madness that drove him to murder. Stanev's farce corrodes any remnants of the grand drama of thinking and theory. With just the chorus and its leader playing all the parts, it does not become very clear who (Raskolnikov? some Messiah? the playwright himself?) is murdering whom (Dostoyevsky's old usurer? a mysterious Sybil? an idea?) and whether the murder ever takes place in a final sort of way or is something repeated ad infinitum. At the very end, the only "persona" envisioned by the directions, the "Messiah," appears as deus ex machina turning the plot into a sort of slaughterhouse *Waiting for Godot* and repeats the "knock, knock, knock" that recurs throughout the play with doors opened to murderers who sometimes seem to be entering and killing, sometimes not. The materialization of the Messiah does not help resolve the question as to who has been knocking all along (the secret police? the dreaming corpse in Moscow? the end of history?): In fact, the Messiah's bloodthirsty "agency" looks like the half-witted excretion of "performance" itself. Thus while the somewhat obtuse chorus, a fairly unflattering representation of the collective intelligence of the seminar, is wondering whether the murder of some unspecified "idea" is not its own inadvertent doing, the play seems to "perform" the butchering of the "idea" through the very operation of its disintegrating language.

So much about the crime. What about the punishment? Is it in the turning of "what's been talked about for too long" into reality? By way of transition to the seminar's legitimate and not so legitimate uses of the "outside," which will be the topic of the next chapter, I will invoke the description of the communist regime as "heterotopias."[50] Unlike utopias, which are imaginary spaces, heterotopias are, according to Foucault, "counter-sites, a kind of effectively enacted utopia in which the real sites, all the other real sites that can be found within the culture, are simultaneously represented, contested, and inverted."[51] For Foucault, the heterotopia is like a mirror, and Bundzhulov emphasizes precisely the function that the communist regime had of mirroring—by "representing, contesting, and inverting"—the structures of "normal societies." This mirroring, it is worth recalling, cannot be adequately studied along the lines of postcolonial othering (although, in trying to adjust to unyielding discursive frames, Eastern intellectuals did resort willy-nilly to postcolonial "subject positions"), but rather along the lines of what Nancy Fraser defined as the "postsocialist" condition: "an absence of any credible overarching emancipatory project."[52] By lamenting this absence Fraser joined the general grief over the fact that the East did not hold up the mirror properly and that, in addition, it let it drop. Between the widespread and admittedly premature rejoicing over the end of history and the no less widespread and no less premature mourning over the end of overarching projects, the ultimate ear into which the impure heterotopic reverberations coalesced turned out to be deaf, after all. Sic transit one of the most massive social experiments in history.

CHAPTER TWO

The West as Intellectual Utopia

The glass is watching us.

—Jorge Luis Borges, "Mirrors"

UTOPIA LOST

Could the lost treasure of the "velvet revolutions" in Eastern Europe be a lost utopia—or, rather, could it be the loss of utopia? Socrates, Plato, and Marsilio Ficino; Foucault and Derrida; Lotman and Mamardashvili coalesced into a single bright star, which, whatever the temporal and geographical odds, shone westward. This was the star of a shimmering lure, of an enticing fantasy: the fantasy of the West as an intellectual (rather than consumerist) utopia. As a specific intellectual experience and, more precisely, as the experience of trying to act out an intellectual utopia, the seminar displays the logic of this fantasy. There it was, *there*, the exclusive inclusiveness of the sharing of knowledge, the passionate circulation of the spirit, the living as an exemplum of the thinking.

I will use the term *utopia*—outside of specific references to utopia as a literary genre or as the philosophical construal of perfect societies—as the capacity to think the placelessness of the nonexistent up to and including the impossible. Seen in this perspective, the seminar—and clearly, at this point the seminar serves as a synecdoche, pars pro toto, of certain Eastern European phantasmatics from the Cold War era—failed. The placeless was thought of as placed, the nowhere was imagined as somewhere. *There.*

That this had been a utopia at all became apparent only after the changes. The nonexistent was lived, at the time when it was lived, as having a place. The difficulty in thinking the nonexistent as placeless is characteristic of the present state of the world at large. As Susan Buck-Morss puts it, "Dreamworlds are not merely illusions. In insisting that what is is not all there is, they are assertions of the human spirit and invaluable politically. . . . But the mere fact of the existence of a different system was proof enough to allow us to think the dream possible."[1] At this point Buck-Morss is speaking about the dreaming to the West of the Iron Curtain. I will look at the dreaming from the other side, the dreaming of the dream. Unlike Buck-Morss, I believe that it is precisely the conflation of dreaming with "the existence of a different system" that deprived the dream of its power. In his late writing, the head of the Moscow-Tartu semiotic school Yuri Lotman deplores the thinking dominated by "veneration for the actualized facts and contempt for what could have but did not become reality."[2] Such a predisposition forecloses the exploration of the "lost paths of history" and remains blind to the cases when "only the irreal has the chance to become a real force."[3] This blindness accompanied utopian visions on both sides of the Iron Curtain. We thought that we were thinking what was. Elsewhere.

UTOPIA AND HETEROTOPIA

The decline of the capacity to think the placelessness of the nonexistent has been attributed to a variety of reasons. According to Foucault's text "Of Other Spaces," it is because of the growing importance of the spatial rather than the temporal dimensions of the world in which we live. "Of Other Spaces" was delivered as a lecture in 1967 but not published until 1984 in French and, in English, 1986. In this sketchy and incomplete but highly suggestive essay, Foucault draws a distinction between utopia and heterotopia in terms of "enactment": Unlike utopias, which "are sites with no real place," heterotopias are "something like counter-sites, a kind of effectively enacted utopia." Like utopias, heterotopias are sites where "the real sites, all the other real sites that can be found within the culture, are simultaneously represented, contested, and inverted."[4] Unlike utopias, heterotopias, the enactments of utopia, are "real."

Foucault does not suggest that heterotopia, which he sees as "formed in the very founding of society," should replace utopia per se. Nonetheless, it is obvious that he is much more interested in heterotopia and that he attaches this interest to his claim that the anxiety of our era has to do fundamentally with space and that we live in an epoch of simultaneity, of juxtaposition, of the near and the far, of the side-by-side, of the dispersed. "Time probably appears to us only as one of the various distributive operations that are possible for the elements that are spread out in space."[5] Later applications of the term confirm this tendency by relating heterotopia to the subsumption of utopia by proliferating spaces that, ultimately, expose a "post-modern" "unfounding of the world."[6] Heterotopia thus comes to designate the disappearance of utopia: The end of utopia is the enactment of utopia. Utopia disappears by turning, from "a site with no real place," into a "counter-site with real place": It disappears by being there; it is not because and insofar as it is. The end of utopia takes the form of the immanence of utopia. In a text that will concern us yet again, Mikhail Ryklin designates this "growth of immanence," marked by the "deficit of the Other," as the "greenhouse" or—for reasons which will become clear later—the "Dubrovnik" effect.[7]

HETEROTOPIAN HOMONYMY

As already mentioned at the end of the previous chapter, drawing on Foucault's text, the Bulgarian sociologist Andrej Bundzhulov offers an analysis of the communist regime (which he calls "socialism") as a "heterotopia." Foucault compares heterotopia to a mirror: I gaze at the mirror in order to find out how I look; by returning the gaze, however, the mirror exerts a countereffect; it influences my stance and prompts me to undertake certain actions with regard to my appearance; that is, it forces me to change in response to it; I become *its* reflection. The mirror image, hence, becomes an agent in the real world; in its turn, it solidifies into existence. In a text that appeared in print later and was not known to us (it was delivered as a radio talk in 1966, a year before "Of Other Spaces") Foucault lists various cases of heterotopia: from the parents' bed turned by playing children into a sea to brothels; from gardens to museums and libraries. In this text, as in the later one, Foucault emphasizes the capacity of heterotopias to *contest* "all other spaces," as well as their propensity to either make the real world illusory, or, indeed, impose their own reality and materialize (Protestant colonies in North America and the Jesuit colony in Paraguay are among his examples). This traffic of reality is, hence, part and parcel of the capacity of heterotopias (for our civilization, Foucault suggests the ship as an example) to act as a reservoir of imagination.[8] There is a poetic and dreamy quality to the earlier text that is no longer there in the later one: It could be because of the genre of the radio talk; or, it could be because Foucault's thought took an altogether different turn and his interest in heterotopias never really took off. It is quite clear, however, that Foucault conceived heterotopias as multiple enclaves within the dominant society. Imposing his concept on the global division during the Cold War, as Bundzhulov did, might seem like overstretching the term's implications in a way not quite truthful to Foucault.

And yet, what interested Bundzhulov was the undeniable propensity of the communist regime to reflect—by "representing, contesting, and inverting"—the structures of Western democracies. From that point of view, a hetrotopia it was. My own contention is that there was a two-way process very much in the manner described by Foucault: that there was a traffic of (ir) reality, which produced reservoirs of imagination and with it, predictable or not that predictable real consequences. CIA support for American abstract expressionism[9] might provide a good example: Abstract expressionism inverts the dogma of socialist realism (realism versus abstraction; class versus individual, objective versus subjective, mimesis versus expression, etc.); it contests ideas about the nature and the purpose of art as well as the claim that the communist society allows free creativity (abstraction was rejected by communist aesthetics, and practicing it was dangerous); and finally, it does all this by reflecting communism's belief in the revolutionary power of art, and, with it, it mirrors the status of art as a matter of interest for the security services. Ultimately, it mimics the hidden strings attached to art's presumed freedom; in fact, it hides them so much better that no one at the time would notice. The effect of this specular encounter can be illustrated by the anecdote of Soviet-Georgian artist Alexander Bandzeladze who "discovered" abstract expressionism by seeing thumbnail black-and-white reproductions and, struck by this revelation, devoted twenty-two years of his life to the illegal clandestine practice of abstractionism.

My point is that the subsumption of utopia (in this case: the utopia of free creativity that communist regimes simultaneously endorsed and did not allow) by heterotopia might explain how, out of its claim to be the end of utopia, communism constituted itself as a utopian locus, which in its turn produced and was ultimately shattered by a utopia projected on the real West. There was, furthermore, a specific linguistic effect of heterotopian mirroring, which I would like to highlight. It caused a lot of confusion in the first decade after the fall of communism, but as a phenomenon it certainly has a wider relevance.

First, another example. I remember the following scene from the London International Festival of the Theatre in 1987: A Ljubljana theater group was invited to join a discussion with the audience, which had been very impressed by the theater's innovative staging of *Medea*. The audience persisted with questions like: Was the message of the performance anti-totalitarian? Was it feminist? Did they have in mind, perhaps, a certain political leader? The creators of the performance unwaveringly answered to all the variants of these questions: We were interested in eternal values; art is not about politics.

Even if we leave aside the dubious practice of flaunting your freedom to people who do not possess it (this is how it looked to me—the grievances that this audience had with Thatcherism did not strike me as even distantly comparable to the Slovenian let alone Bulgarian situation at this moment), there is a further point to make about this scene of misunderstanding: At the time, "eternal values" signified a viable political stance in the Eastern bloc countries, and, then as now, an art refusing to be political might still make political sense in a situation where the political is trivialized and made senseless through its very omnipresence. "Eternal values," hence, meant different things to the two sides in this exchange: on the one side, *opposition* (to the topical political propaganda expected from "socialist" art); on the other side, *compliance* (to conservative norms masking their topical interests as timeless). This hidden semantic inversion and the "contestation" of divergent meanings went unrecognized—both sides felt the other side was resorting to clichés; the result was disappointment and boredom.

As my example demonstrates, the discursive effects of heterotopian mirroring were there while the Iron Curtain existed. And yet, they became painfully effective only after the changes when the mirror was shattered. One of the ironies of postcommunism was the influx of literal terminological and rhetorical repetitions, which came from different sections of the Western political spectrum and which had to offer the language of a totally new situation. For example, the end of communism was hailed (or mourned) as "the end of history" and the "end of utopia." However, the very coming into being of communist regimes was articulated as the triumph of science over utopia: The regimes described their implementation as the end of utopia, which took humanity on the road to the end of history. Thus both the implementation and the fall of communism were wrapped up as the end of utopia and the end of history. What was meant to designate the new situation was homonymous to the designation of the old situation.

Such strange turns provoked debates only in some cases. The question of public and private space discussed in the previous chapter was such a case. It was at the center of some East-West debates on feminism, which took place in the first years of the transition. In these debates, the Western side usually criticizes and the Eastern side usually defends private space—claiming, on the one hand, that, by offering resources for resistance and personal freedom, private space played a crucial political role during communism and pointing out, on the other, that the contention that "the personal is political" had different implications in view of a "political" that infiltrated the private sphere by recruiting armies of informers reporting on their colleagues, friends, and family.

The same applies to the claim that science and all forms of knowledge are political: Such a claim looked hazardous against the background of the ideologically motivated bans that had been imposed on (and in certain cases subsequently lifted from) a number of disciplines or theories in Eastern Europe. The very history of the "softening" of the regime might, in fact, be described as the gradual negotiation for larger and larger territories to be recognized as nonpolitical and hence open for free articulation.

The conflation of the work of artists and thinkers with their biography or the rejection of their oeuvre as a whole because certain parts of it were not politically correct looked even worse: The denunciation of Paul de Man as a fascist collaborator, which coincided with the beginning of the changes, had an uncanny flavor in the East European context of harassment of intellectuals. The type of feminists who had nothing to tell us but that we wore unacceptable heels conjured up the ghost of the communist militia that busied itself with the length of skirts and hair (at the beginning of the 1960s people in Bulgaria were sent to prison camps for wearing the wrong clothes). The list can be extended.

The communicative crisis of a conference in Dubrovnik (this fascinating Croatian city became, in the 1980s, an important East-meets-West academic center) offers, through the commentaries of some of its participants, a rather dramatic illustration of the problem. A number of Bulgarian "Seminar" figures attended this conference, which took place in 1990. Fredric Jameson and the charismatic Russian-Georgian philosopher Merab Mamardashvili were at the center of attention, although in rather different ways: While Yugoslavian television arrived on the first day to interview Fredric Jameson, Mamardashvili commanded a considerable appeal among East European intellectuals, which, in a manner typical of communist times, had nothing to do with the media or with official ranking. Susan Buck-Morss, who was one of the organizers of the conference, writes about it in her study of the twentieth century, *Dreamworld and Catastrophe: The Passing of Mass Utopia in East and West.* In what seems to have been the climax of growing misunderstanding, Mamardashvili grabbed a piece of chalk from Buck-Morss's hand in a manner that she describes as gentle and yet phallic from the point of view of both gender and age.[10] The collision of gender relations with power relations brought her to the boiling point, she remarks. What was the conflict about apart from the general confusion Buck-Morss so vividly describes? Everybody I talked to remembered the gesture; no one remembered the issue. Buck-Morss writes nothing about the specific issue that was so much in need of a piece of chalk either. It is as if the words had evaporated and transformed the encounter into a silent movie scene. There was another wordless crisis. Fredric Jameson left the conference earlier than planned and without warning: Being one of the organizers of the conference, Buck-Morss had to phone the hotel (Mikhail Ryklin, who also attended the conference, notes that Jameson, the fighter against imperialism, was the only one who stayed at the "Imperial" hotel, while most of the Eastern European fighters for a free market economy stayed at a dormitory)[11] and find out in this way that Jameson had left.

Even leaving these two inarticulate events aside, the conference seems to have been a devastating experience for a number of the participants. Ryklin speaks of "painful clashes" and treats Dubrovnik as an emblem of the post–Cold War "global warming," marked by the "deficit of the Other"—in fact, he uses "greenhouse effect" and "Dubrovnik effect" as synonyms.[12] Almost ten years later, in an issue of a Moscow art journal devoted to a recapitulation of the "murky image" of the 1990s, Elena Petrovskaia singles out this conference as the only concrete narrative in a decade of speechless and traumatic flux. She says nothing about Mamardashvili's chalk or Jameson's leaving. She notes, instead, that the "individual hopes for a broadening of the international dialogue turned into a deep disappointment for both sides" and that "what began as a search for togetherness ended in complete isolation." The "euphoria of finally achieved freedom" was replaced by an awareness that the fall of the Iron Curtain did not lead to an increase in mutual understanding.[13] Singling out the Bulgarian participants, Petrorvskaia notes the much larger multiplicity and plurality of Eastern European languages and perspectives. At the time no one realized that this plurality of perspectives was the fragile offspring of a revolutionary moment and that immediately after the changes it would be ruthlessly forced, Petrovskaia says, into two categories: convertible discourses and autistic discourses. In less than a decade the hopes hardened into fossils: "While still alive, we have been turned into mummies."[14]

There was one even more extreme response to the "Dubrovnik effect." Bulgarian art critic Luchezar Boiadjiev told me that at this conference he decided to give up theory altogether. Via conceptual art, he turned to the language of project proposals, the quintessence of convertible discourses. "In terms of convertibility, nothing can beat money, not art for sure"—he noted in a discussion. Or, as Susan Buck-Morss puts it in her "Letter from New York," published immediately after Petrovskaia's mournful account of the 1990s, no one is interested in Russian culture any more because "the devaluation of the ruble, which gives rise to the social insecurity of broad sectors of society, including the intelligentsia and the artists . . . makes equal cultural exchange impossible."[15]

And yet, what happened in Dubrovnik? The ruble was not devalued at the time. Was it a revelation of the globalized "deficit of the Other," as Ryklin would have it—somewhat literally illustrated by Jameson's abrupt departure and, a month later, by Mamardashvili's sudden death in an airport? Or was it, on the contrary, a matter of cultural difference, a "clash between Eastern 'messianism' and Western 'professionalism,'" as Ivaylo Ditchev, another Bulgarian participant in the conference, wrote to me? Although Jameson does not say so, Buck-Morss believes that he refers to this conference when he writes that "the more their [i.e., postcommunist Easterners'] truths are couched in Orwellian language, the more tedious they become to us; the more our truths demand expression in even the weakest forms of Marxian language—that of simple social democracy say, or even the welfare state or social justice, or equality—the more immediately the Eastern hearing aids get switched off. . . . There are really no common denominations in this initial struggle [between East and West] for discursive rules, and what we end up with is the inevitable comedy of each side muttering irrelevant replies in its own favorite language."[16]

The problem, as demonstrated in Buck-Morss's account and as indicated by Jameson's somewhat irritable description, does not spring from not understanding the language that the other side is using. It does not seem to be a problem of too little, or too much, alterity. It seems, rather, to be a problem of some sort of spooky amalgam of sameness and alterity, which might be described as "homonymy." The Dubrovnik crisis can be seen as arising from the traffic of homonymous concepts. Going back to the description of the regime as the "heterotopia" of Western democracies, we could designate this homonymy as "heterotopian." Heterotopian homonyms are not simply identically sounding words with this or that different meaning. As in Foucault's specular definition of heterotopia, heterotopian homonyms, while ostensibly identical, in fact "represent, contest, and invert" each other.

What happens, then, is that while being transmitted between their interlocutors the respective utterances get transformed from something that makes sense to boredom—to a triviality that says nothing precisely because what it says looks so very familiar. The very comprehensibility of the said produces incomprehension and even deafness (the metaphor about switching off one's hearing aids was a common way to describe resistance to ideological pressure in the East). The messages are not heard precisely to the extent that they look familiar. Their very familiarity—concealing the inversion and contestation that goes together with the mirror imaging—precludes the margin of incomprehension which drives communication. As Yuri Lotman puts it, "In communication, our interest lies precisely in the situation that makes communication difficult and even impossible."[17] Instead of turning toward the incomprehensibility of comprehensibility—since incomprehensibility appears here as boredom and deafness at the very heart of comprehensibility—the complaint about the lack of "common denominations" (which, to say it once again, is not simply a lack but a heterotopian inversion and contestation thereof) focuses on the "initial struggle" as to who will determine the discursive rules. By giving up speaking and by leaving, Jameson performatively demonstrated who would determine them: not me, the system.

The Dubrovnik conference seems to have captured the very moment of the disappearance of the mirror. Once the mirror falls to pieces and the heterotopian spaces on its two sides expose their immanence to each other, the discursive outcome is neutralizing or even deadly. This neutralization could be seen in the case of the public/private debate—instead of producing a new perspective, the debate evacuated the problem itself. The unacknowledged homonymy did not provoke a dialogic rearticulation; instead, it resulted in a desemanticization of the signifiers. One might presume that this evacuation of meaning was one of the unrecognized factors of the rhetorical scarcity which became apparent during the messy Yugoslav wars and which migrated to other conflicts, as bloody as they are inarticulate. It was as if it were no longer possible to "formulate a discourse of freedom appropriate to contesting contemporary antidemocratic configurations of power."[18] The perception that the disintegration of communism has not brought about the hoped-for discursive transformation, that the post-totalitarian epoch tends to unconsciously repeat and quote the ancien régime, that, with the "dark opposite of liberalism gone," as Wendy Brown's analyses spell out, the " 'instinct for freedom turned back on itself' [has surfaced] in the form of a cultural ethos and politics of reproach, rancor, moralism, and guilt,"[19] and the "least defensible elements of twentieth-century communist states, leaving aside overt and routinized political repression, have . . . made their appearance" in the old democracies;[20] the perception, that is, that the "ban on thinking"[21] has been simply reconfigured and, in fact, implemented in a more cunning repressive machine, may find some explanation in the light of this terminological entropy.

One of the vexing consequences of heterotopian homonymy is the impossibility of naming the previous regime. It called itself socialism, but this is a term that clearly does not fit its Western usages, usages that are struggling to survive the collapse of the Eastern bloc. The regime's enemies and critics called it communism, which is also, in view of proper definitions of the term, a misnomer: The ideologues of the former regime were right in disclaiming its application to any existing order. Neither was it a totalitarian regime proper after the demise of Stalin. There is no name that would create consensus across the various countries that made up the Soviet bloc, let alone individual thinkers or politicians, or, indeed, everyday language users. My calling it "the communist regime" has to be accepted together with my awareness of the unsatisfactory and provisional nature of this designation. Clumsily, it has to evoke both the condemnation of this drastic social experiment and the understanding of its complicated nature both in itself and as a factor in a global economy of critical and projective thinking.

THE UTOPIA OF UTOPIA

Whatever happened at that particular Dubrovnik conference, it served, for Ryklin, as a fit parable for the "deficit of the Other." It provided sufficient reason for Luchezar Boiadjiev's giving up on the "autism" of his prior theoretical existence. It provided the background to Petrovskaia's claim that "while still living, we have been turned into mummies." Against this background Mamardashvili's sudden death in an airport just a month after the conference appears as the ultimate representation of the "Dubrovnik effect." Some became convertible; the less convertible became depressive; the inconvertible died: This is, in sum, the story of the Eastern European transition. Referring to Mamardashvili's death, Buck-Morss is prone to assume that when he grabbed the chalk from her hand Mamardashvili "insisted on the critical, repeated task of philosophical questioning itself, the necessity always to begin again," and, perhaps, warned us of the "danger of dismissing the responsibilities of thinking through the complexities of the present."[22] And, indeed, through what he describes as "acts of philosophizing," Mamardashvili claims in his works that "dead knowledge is of no importance to us—we turn to the past and we understand it only to the degree that we can restore what used to be thought in our own capacity to think and in what we can think now."[23]

The question is why, while the Western side mourned the loss of bulky entities like "the existence of a different system," it was precisely the "painful clashes" in a seminar room that caused so much drama on the Eastern side? Why was this small-scale classroom fiasco—nothing like the grand "absence of any credible overarching emancipatory project"[24]—experienced so excruciatingly, so traumatically by Easterners? Why did the wreckage of "individual hopes for a broadening of the international dialogue" appear as the sufficient explanation for melancholy, autism, live mummification, premature death? What dreamworld collapsed under the ruins of a piece of chalk?

One year before this Dubrovnik conference its future Bulgarian participants took part in a panel at one of the last seminars before the changes. This panel, knowingly or not, tried to name the collapsing dream. It was called "classical space" and was opposed—in a rather carnivalesque manner—to the post-modern space whose defenders at this forum admitted later that they shared the same "classical" illusions. The fantasy of classical space places intellectual discussions—the conversation of the world—in a uniform container where anyone can participate on equal terms. This fantasy disregards hierarchies, schools, geopolitical, cultural, linguistic, disciplinary, or methodological differentiations, political incommensurabilities, the resistance to theory, personal rivalries, the curvings of space caused by academic positions, which curve other curvings . . . let alone the devaluation of the ruble. The fantasy, whose patron saint might very well be Marsilio Ficino, is supported by the practice of a "philosophical form of life" (exemplified by Merab Mamardashvili) and by what I described apropos of the seminar as "the embrace of living and thinking in the *phonē*." What was the logic of the dreaming? Was this space in fact classical? Why did Eastern European intellectuals project it onto the West?

WHICH IS PRIMARY, MATTER OR CONSCIOUSNESS?

In 1982 a group of Sofia University philosophy undergraduates was on an exchange visit to Moscow University. They were all lodged in the same building. One of the students was a Marxist (as they were all supposed to be) and a nondrinker; the rest would drink and talk late into the night. This is how they hit upon the idea of breaking into the room of the Marxist, who, at two o'clock in the morning, was sleeping peacefully, and of shaking him violently awake to answer urgently the question: "Which is primary, matter or consciousness?"

This somewhat cruel philosophical performance was aimed at the "fundamental" question of dialectical materialism. The question had only one correct answer, which a true Marxist (this was the joke) was expected to remember even while sleeping: Matter was primary; consciousness was secondary. The primacy of matter provided the ontological grounding for the primacy of the base (productive forces and relations of production) over the superstructure (culture, science, religion); the primacy of labor over thinking, of the worker over the philosopher, and of "stormy, practical life" over the vita contemplativa. The students' joke, however, apart from targeting dogmatic slumbers, unwittingly performed one of the paradoxes of the functioning of Marxism as an official ideology: Matter might or might not be primary, and yet the questioning of this primacy undoubtedly required a vigilance of consciousness that one could never relinquish—certainly not while sleeping!

The tension that becomes apparent in the requirement for this relentless vigilance was manifested in Marx's endlessly discussed eleventh thesis on Feuerbach: "The philosophers have only interpreted the world, in various ways; the point is to change it." It is important to change rather than explain the world—or it is important to change and not simply explain the world. Surely, the world should be changed—but by whom? By the proletariat? Why then address the philosophers? The Marxian invocation to philosophers poses the philosophers' occupation—thinking—as bound up with the proletarian transformation of the world. The result is a simultaneous mobilization and rejection of thinking.

It is not necessary to evoke here the history of concrete cases where the exalted inevitability of intellectuals was repeatedly shaken by attempts at their complete annihilation. Although the regime implemented its power as monodiscursive truth through the discouragement and, frequently, the physical repression of thinking and of those who were appointed to exercise it in relentless vigilance, certain inherent tensions of Marxism, on which the monodiscursivity was based, shored up and, in fact, required the constant exercise of the capacity to think. One might say that the primary scene of the regime—its theoretical origin—predetermined the return of the repressed that would ultimately prove fatal for its existence.

SPUTNIK

One of the spectacular expressions of this propensity of Marxism was the difficulty the regime had in dealing with extreme forms of hubristic revolt that were nourished by "scientific materialist" resentment against the material limits of human existence. Will humanity be able to become aware of itself as part of the universe? Transform its nature through consciously directed "active evolution"? Modify the physical world to fit human moral requirements? Leave the cradle of the Earth to settle other planets within and beyond the solar system? Attain immortality and turn into a cosmogonic factor that will bring the blind injustice of nature under control? "Thought is not a form of energy. How can it change material processes?"—asked biogeochemist Vladimir Vernadksy in 1942.[25] Vernadsky's name became associated, first, with the idea of the biosphere, and, later on, with the idea of a noosphere: the noosphere envisions the metamorphosis of reason into a geological factor (with what degree of immediacy is a question of ongoing debates). And indeed, how could one reject, on the basis of "scientific Marxism," the idea of human thought being able to "work" the "anthropocosmization" of the universe? Of human thought being or, perhaps, becoming an immediate material force of planetary, stellar, and galactic proportions? Was not the invocation to philosophers to change the world?

Since the middle of the nineteenth century, such questioning informed the thinking of a number of scientists, philosophers, and artists in Russia and, later, the Soviet Union. It came to be designated as "Russian cosmism." The radical questions of Russian cosmism, driven by a paradoxical materialist nausea with materiality and animated by a rebellious agenda for the redemption of the "inferno" of "laboring matter" through the grace of human intelligence, were impelled by the conviction that natural laws were intolerable. They condemned human beings to biological wretchedness. They bound them to the ultimate evil, gravity. They subjected them to time. Can future universal harmony redeem past—or even present, the one taking place right now—suffering? This aporia looms large in Dostoevsky's work where it is articulated in all its terror. Can we accept a perfect society if it costs the tears of even one abused child? Even if these tears were shed centuries ago?

The impasse of this query, which survived all the way from Dostoyevsky to the Soviet paleontologist and science fiction writer Ivan Yefremov, seems to have originated with Nikolai Fyodorov, the founder of Russian cosmism. Fyodorov chose to spend his life as an obscure librarian in Moscow and refused to publish (his works were published posthumously by his followers), but he exerted an enormous influence upon many of his illustrious contemporaries. With Fyodorov this extreme question brought an extreme solution: a project that he called "repatrification" and that demanded nothing more or less than the scientific rearrangement of the molecules of the universe in such a manner that all fathers, everybody and anybody who ever lived but especially the fathers, should be resurrected—in the flesh.

There is a heartrending and a rather mystifying aspect to this "repatrification" tale, where Fyodorov, an illegitimate child of a certain prince Gagarin, appears—because of the role he played for the Soviet space doctrine—as the spiritual predecessor of . . . the first cosmonaut Gagarin (a descendant of the selfsame prince!). And yet, if the "repatrification" marks the hidden pain that provoked the fatherless child into visions of leaving the sad Earth behind and transforming the cosmos into the everlasting body of the living fathers, many of his ideas, including his obsession with the inevitability of spreading the human race throughout the universe, were taken over by his followers. A number of studies have followed the line that leads from Fydorov to the founder of Russian cosmonautics, Konstantin Tsiolkovsky (1857–1935). Isolated from the world and impeded in his school education because of his deafness, Tsiolkovsky, while reading in the library where Fyodorov worked, was provided by him with an individual curriculum. Tsiolkovsky, in his turn, leads us to the major figure in the Soviet space program, constructor Sergei Korolyov (1907–1966) and hence to the era of space exploration.[26]

The regime dealt with the contemporary representatives of cosmism in its characteristic manner: some of them were shot dead (P. A. Florensky and N. A. Setnitsky); some died in exile (V. N. Muravyov and A. K. Gorsky); some spent years in prisons and camps (sixteen years in the case of A. L. Chizhevsky). Others, however, were allowed to die peacefully (as did Vernadsky who had to witness the loss of university autonomy two times under two different regimes and who was declared at some point to be the "banner of reactionary forces"), and still others (among them, the self-taught Tsiolkovsky, who was ignored by official science before the revolution) were lavishly given resources to propagate their ideas and thus reach the "real thing" as exemplified by Sergei Korolyov. Korolyov, in his turn, with all his obvious contributions to the military, was sentenced to ten years incarceration in 1938 (the war modified this imprisonment at an unspecified moment); and Yefremov, although he was recognized as a major official writer, had his apartment searched by the KGB immediately after his death in 1972 (notably, long after Stalin was gone).

In any case, there is a direct link from Fyodorov to the symbolic event of the Cold War—the appearance of the first Soviet artificial satellites that began to pierce the sky above Manhattan, rivaling Sirius with their "yellow-white brilliance."[27] The magnitude of this event—"second in importance to no other, not even to the splitting of the atom," as Hannah Arendt put it[28]—cannot be reduced to the Stalinist modernization project, or to pragmatic—be they military or consumerist—concerns. Sputnik, subtended as it was by cosmic messianism and by the project of leaving the Earth and never coming back, demonstrated the power of "consciousness" over "blind matter." There was an exorbitance to it, a surplus, excess. There it was, the superstructure, whose relative independence from the base had to account for the premature existence of the communist system, on its way to infinity.

The manner in which Russian cosmism was inscribed in the Marxist ideology of the communist regime was discussed in a variety of contending perspectives at the seminars in Bulgaria during the 1980s. Although Vladislav Todorov differentiates between Marx's "horizontal geographical utopia" and Fyodorov's "cosmic vertical utopia" with its thrust to "inseminate" the universe,[29] he sees them nevertheless as part and parcel of the modernist insanity of the regime qua Marxist regime. Ivaylo Ditchev, for whom Fyodorov's views represent a "strange mixture of rightist Orthodox messianism and leftist utopian eschatologism,"[30] is prone to see them as a deviation from Marxism. Hence Ditchev feels "tempted to ask whether Soviet communism was not closer to Fyodorov than to Marx."[31] My belief is that cosmism exemplifies the paradox I already referred to. The totalitarianism of the communist regime is eroded by the teaching through which it tries to implement itself. It is a self-defeating idea to turn a philosophy, that is, a thinking conscious of its thinking, into the one truth. Sooner or later such an idea will work—that is, think—against itself. The thinking that the regime paradoxically encouraged inevitably turned against the limitations on thinking that it was expected to impose. The devious, incongruous, often comic, and yet defiant and ultimately productive infiltration of communism by cosmism (especially drastically enacted in Bulgaria through the political career and the mysterious death of the dictator's daughter, Lyudmila Zhivkova) became possible thanks to the irresistible, although repeatedly repressed, healthy side of the regime: its inability to stop encouraging what it was trying to terminate. Cosmism was a symptom of this inability: It was about dissatisfaction with what was; it insisted on the status of humanity as an unfinished project; it demanded "active evolution," it was restless and dynamic. It was not an attitude that could be expected to nurture docile subjects. And, in spite of the repressions, it could not be contained and found its way into the official institutions.

AN ASIDE ON SCIENCE FICTION, SCIENCE FICTION CLUBS, AND SECRET AGENTS

At the end of the 1970s, when I began frequenting the Ivan Yefremov club in Sofia, science fiction clubs had been established in many of the bigger cities as part of the Youth Cultural Centers run by the Organization of Communist Youth. The frequenters of the clubs were mostly high school students and undergraduates but people in their thirties and forties or older were not that uncommon. These clubs had the tendency, which was also characteristic of the seminars during the 1980s, to move toward larger public spaces (conferences and conventions on a national level) and simultaneously to invade private spaces and private life. Although, unlike the seminars, the clubs had no professional basis, they trod the same borderline between oral discussion and written text: The exchange of such communications formed the ethos of the clubs' togetherness. In the 1980s, the Sofia club published a number of collections on the verge between samizdat and official publishing and, after the fall of communism, some of its frequenters did emerge as professional writers and publishers.

In the spring of 1989 when the secret services grew desperate at the prospect of the imminent collapse of the regime, of which they were probably more aware than anybody else, I was approached by an officer from the so-called Sixth Department, the one dealing with intellectuals, who, it turned out, was in charge of science fiction and science fiction clubs and—although I had stopped visiting these clubs for almost ten years—in charge of me. We met in a café called—of all things—Prague. Insofar as no clear purpose for this meeting became apparent—unless we assume such a purpose to be the officer's polite intellectual interest in recent developments in American science fiction—I believe this interview was (a) part of an intimidation campaign meant to remind us of a detail we were beginning to forget—that we were observed; and (b) an attempt on the part of the services to demonstrate to whoever oversaw and directed their actions that they were trying to do something. The practice of political blackmailing during the 1990s hints at a third, more sinister purpose: the creation of seedy dossiers for as many people as possible. In any case, many intellectuals were approached by the services for the first and, as chance would have it, last time in this last year of the regime.

In her seminal analysis of opposition and dissidence in Bulgaria during communism Dimitrina Petrova—who was asked for an interview in 1985 and, unlike me, was asked to go to the offices of the Sixth Department, a rather scarier invitation—notes that the destruction of the "myth surrounding the security services' omnipotence"[32] was a major achievement of the 1980s. In her text, Petrova recounts the striking strategy of how to behave toward the "organs" that was elaborated by Krassimir Kanev, the very unorthodox Marxist whom the drinking party in Moscow woke up to check whether he kept thinking while sleeping.[33] Petrova points out, however, that only Sofia intellectuals, probably due to the network of connections established between them, had gained this relative freedom vis-à-vis the security services, and that outside of Sofia, even in the 1980s, repression took drastic forms. I keep pondering why I was not transferred from my youthful science fiction "supervisor" to those taking care of university affiliations. It was, perhaps, a bad sign of my . . . subversiveness. Today I am less surprised, however, than I was at the time about science fiction clubs being an object of specialized scrutiny.

The most obvious but also the least interesting explanation would be that, by placing events on other planets, science fiction could criticize obliquely the existing order: utopias, by presenting what was supposed to happen but did not; anti-utopias, by depicting extraterrestrial totalitarian regimes suspiciously resembling earthly realities. And yet, the apprehensions of the regime about science fiction did not primarily concern, I believe, its allegorical repertoire. Much greater uneasiness must have ensued from its strategic potential: by being "scientific," science fiction agglutinated itself, so to speak, to the freedom from ideological control that the sciences had already won. This was the strategy of the humanities all along, up to Epstein's idea of creating a "cultural laboratory"[34] and Podoroga's Laboratory for the Study of Post-Classical Philosophy, Literature, and Art, which exists to this very day.[35] This was the reason why theories with a structuralist or any other orientation claiming scientificity were at all possible, even if only marginally.[36] As a hybrid between "science" and "fiction," between the sciences and the humanities, science fiction created an example and a bridge for the further clearance from political control of the humanities, as well as literature and the arts.

To add a further nuance to the paradoxes of the regime, the censorship that restricted science-fiction publishing exerted a quality control that turned the austerely selected field into an area of high-minded questioning rather than one of entertainment and phantasmatic contentment. This is the ironic background to Stanislaw Lem's complaints about what the market did to American science fiction.

> The fact that a domestication of the cosmos has taken place, a diminution that whisked away those eternally silent abysses of which Pascal spoke with horror, is masked in science fiction by the blood that is so literally spilled in its pages. . . . losing thereby that indifference [of the nonhuman universe] which causes man to project new enigmas to be solved and new secrets to be lifted, in the vain hope to get there the answer to the question of his own meaning.[37]

I cannot resist the temptation to record the appearance of the intelligence services at this end of the story, too. Lem admired the disturbing antifoundationalist vision of Philip K. Dick's best writing and called him "a visionary among the charlatans."[38] Lem had no way of knowing that Dick repeatedly wrote letters that denounced him to the FBI and described him as a "faceless group from Crakow" bent on destroying American science fiction. The FBI probably ignored these clear products of paranoia. Yet it appears that Dick had been approached by the services in his youth—similar occurrences tilted, in the East, psyches far more stable than his.[39]

As for the science fiction clubs, a cheerful nonchalance about informers was, given the times, a symptom of psychic health. As a collectivity, the science fiction clubs, like the seminars in the 1980s, allowed no conjectures that would dampen the conversations. Like the theory that became the medium of the seminars, science fiction was interdisciplinary, transferable, and translatable; it was not tied to particularized identities; it could cross borders; it could be entered from different political, disciplinary and personal positions; it was interactive and open to debate. It voiced dissatisfaction with what is.

THE FANTASY

In 1929—after Vernadsky introduced the term "biosphere" and before he turned to the conceptual potential of the term "noosphere"—P. A. Florensky came up with the idea of a "pneumatosphere," which he described in a letter to Vernadsky: "As for myself, I would like to express an idea that needs concrete argumentation and is as yet just a heuristic beginning. The idea is that in, or perhaps on, the biosphere there exists something that could be called pneumatosphere, that is, a specific type of substance, which takes part in the circulation of culture or, rather, the circulation of the spirit."[40]

The idea that "culture" and "spirit" are the circulation of "part of the substance" of the biosphere was taken up and elaborated in the semiotic theory of Yuri Lotman. Seen from the perspective of thinking worlds (the English title of Lotman's book *Universe of the Mind* appears in Russian as "within thinking worlds," *Vnutri misliashchih mirov*), Lotman's theory emerges as a transmutation—or, to use a term to which he gave considerable weight, translation—of cosmism. Lotman's semiosphere, which he justifiably relates to Vernadsky's noosphere, is a collective nous that thinks itself into existence through processes of signification that appear to be automatic, suprasubjective, and inexorable. Transected by numerous boundaries of intensified semiotization, traversed by messages that, moving across borders, must be incessantly translated and transmitted, the semiosphere is beyond individual but also beyond totalitarian control. It moves like a huge celestial body in semiotic space, where it clashes with other semiospheres and with the remnants—the comets—of former, now dead semiospheres. Furthermore, it is not closed in on itself: it can explode and thus open "semiotic windows" toward the nonsemiotic, parts of which it can suck in while casting out its own dead contents back into the nonsemiotizable. The semiosphere "seethes like the sun; clusters of activity boil up in different places, in the depths and on the surface, irradiating relatively peaceful areas with its immense energy. But unlike that of the sun, the energy of the semiosphere is the energy of information, the energy of thought."[41]

This description of the semiosphere is strikingly similar to the thinking ocean in Stanislaw Lem's novel *Solaris*, which was rendered by Tarkovsky in a remarkable film version. The idea of the noosphere is presented in *Solaris* literally as a brain the size of a planet. It controls its cosmic environment and enters into a strange sort of "dialogue" with the humans who try—with various degrees of goodwill and, ultimately, with dubious success—to understand this immense and lonely brooding. Skeptical as he is about the "vain hope" of finding human meaning in "the eternally silent abysses of which Pascal spoke with horror," Lem nevertheless presents a vista of the "anthropocosmic" dimension of thinking. If I turned to this vista, the vista of cosmism, in my attempt to create a narrative about the *illusions perdues* of yet another lost generation, it was in order to delineate the "dreamworld," which formed its utopian horizon. What emerges is the construction of an imaginary global *nous*. This fantasy—whose theoretical ramifications were suggested initially by Vernadsky's noosphere and were later elaborated by Lotman's semiosphere and whose powerful artistic representation was offered by the thinking ocean in Lem's novel and in Tarkovsky's film—the fantasy, that is, of a planetary mind "seething like the sun" and bent on the tireless translation of its "clusters of activity" into new thought, became a fantasy at the precise point of its forgetfulness that it was a *topos outopos*, a placeless place, a utopia. This was the point where the fantasy fused with the vision of the West not as a land of freedom and not as a land of plenty (these topics are a different matter) but of the West as a land of the *obzhivyan* undeath of intellectuality. There it was, the fantastic ocean of unfathomable, impenetrable, mysterious and yet powerfully effective thinking. As in Dante's *Limbo*, where he meets the illustrious shades of Antiquity to whom, through the very imaginary act of meeting them, he conjoins his own poetic fate but also the future fate of the West, there it was, the land where the conversation of humanity had sustained, uninterrupted throughout the centuries, its lofty whisperings. It would be enough to get rid of the beasts standing in our way for us to join in.

The ironies of the disillusionment surfaced in the following epiphany. A philosopher from the group of students who woke up the slumbering Marxist to check whether he kept thinking his philosophical riddles while dreaming joined a North American PhD program immediately after the fall of communism. On a gray rainy afternoon he was walking toward his department when he spotted two of his most cherished professors standing in front of the neo-gothic building, engaged in what seemed to be an engrossing conversation. "Whatever important philosophical dilemma are these two excellent men debating?"—he wondered, admiring the sight, with visions of Raphael's "School of Athens" in his head, Plato raising his hand toward the sky and Aristotle checking his zeal with a well-measured horizontal gesture. He drew closer. The discussion was about insurance companies.

HETEROTOPIA REVISITED

Foucault invokes the mirror as a mixed experience of utopia and heterotopia in order to illustrate the difference between the two. I gaze at the nowhere (my image in the mirror); by gazing at me—by returning the gaze, the way my image in the mirror returns my gaze—the nowhere "exerts a sort of counteraction on the position that I occupy" and thus solidifies into existence.

Utopia, like the reflection in the mirror, is a "placeless place" that allows me to see myself where I am not. Heterotopia is the transformation of the gaze that comes from the mirror into a material power that forces me to "reconstitute myself there where I am." In contradistinction to utopia, heterotopia has a normalizing function and facilitates disciplinary procedures on this side of the mirror.

In his analysis of the communist system as the heterotopia of "normal societies," Bundzhulov refers to Jorge Luis Borges' "Tlön, Uqbar, Orbis Tertius."[42] This reference draws attention to the fact that the mirror would not be sufficient to explain the communist heterotopia and that what we need, rather, is a "conjunction of a mirror and an encyclopedia."[43] Bundzhulov ignores a certain aspect that seems to have been important to Borges: Through the words of "one of the heresiarchs of Uqbar," Borges asserts that "mirrors and copulation are abominable, because they increase the number of men."[44] There is, therefore, a resemblance between copulation and the conjunction of the mirror and the encyclopedia. Unlike copulation, however, the conjunction of the mirror and the encyclopedia presupposes the hubris of proving to a "nonexistent God that mortal man was capable of conceiving a world." And indeed, in Borges' story, men are increased wholesale, by entire worlds. It is in one of these worlds, brought into being by a "secret society of astronomers, biologists, engineers, metaphysicians, poets, chemists, algebraists, moralists, painters, geometers"—brought into being, that is, "through the rigor of chess masters, not of angels"—that the Uqbar heresiarch, poor looking-glass creature that he is, pronounces the abomination of mirrors.

The concept of heterotopia provides a unique entrance to the analysis of the mirroring effects in the geopolitical deployments of power, so amply exemplified by the history of the Cold War. In this case, however, I am interested in its potential for diagnosing our own lost utopia. Children of a mirror and an encyclopedia that we were, we thought we were gazing at *the place*. It turned out to be another mirror after all.

CHAPTER THREE

Between Irony and Revolution: Sexual Difference and the Case of *Aufhebung*

DOWN WITH HEAVEN: MATERIALISM

Among its various meanings, *Aufhebung* signifies, on the one hand, annulment, destruction, cancellation and, on the other, preservation, conservation. In his reflections on the term, Hegel points out the word's capacity to embrace precisely these two opposite sets of meanings, turning this capacity into an example of the unique philosophical advantages and the "speculative spirit" of the German language. As Derrida, who had a great deal to say about the *Aufhebung*, notes, according to Hegel this is "the speculative concept par excellence . . . , the concept whose untranslatable privilege is wielded by the German language."[1] This privilege, furthermore, is attributed by Hegel to the proximity between philosophical and everyday language: Even when foreign words have been adopted into German—and his own—philosophy, they are the kind of words that have earned, through frequent usage, the right to German citizenship.

Given Hegel's emphasis on the connection between thinking and language and on the intrinsic Germanness of *Aufhebung*, it is not surprising that in English and, more dramatically, in

French, discussions of the import and meaning of this term have frequently been bound up with debates about its translation. One would be tempted to say "unavoidably bound up." Yet this turns out not to be the case. In Russia, there seem to have been no such debates. Ever since early in the nineteenth century up to the last decades of the twentieth century, the rendering of *Aufhebung* as *snaytie* and of *aufheben* as *snyat'* has not only been widely functioning in philosophical contexts but it has also imported a Hegelian slant into the everyday usage of the word, turning into a commonplace the idea that the dialectical "unity and struggle of opposites" marking each and every phenomenon has its natural course in their simultaneous destruction and preservation.

It should be noted at this point that the smooth assumption of the term was part of the massive, ardent, quite early, and, sometimes it has been claimed, fateful reception of Hegel's philosophy in Russia, which turned Hegel into a "living dramatis persona in the history of nineteenth-century [Russian] thinking"[2] and, even more strongly put, into "Russia's destiny."[3] Ivan Kireevskyi, probably the first Russian to attend Hegel's lectures, writes in the 1840s that everybody in Russia speaks in a Hegelian language because "it is in the air we breathe."[4] Since the reception of Hegel more or less coincided with the reception of French utopianism, the encounter of these two trends was perceived by nineteenth-century thinkers (Belinskyi, Hertsen, Bakunin, Chernishevskyi) as facilitating the union of science and revolution, thus allowing socialist ideas to acquire during the 1840s their "firm foundation" in the principles of Hegel's philosophy.[5] This specific configuration of revolutionary and philosophical currents explains why, on the one hand, during the Stalin era it could be asserted that "the proletariat is the only inheritor to whatever is vital and creative in Hegel's philosophy,"[6] while, on the other, nowadays it can be argued that, although not intrinsically responsible for this, "Hegel's system is the substantial cause for the demonism of the revolutionary epoch."[7]

There is a certain logic, therefore, to the fact that the basic meanings of *snyat'* and *snyatie* involve taking or bringing down. They may refer to the more or less decisive or energetic removal of barriers, obstacles, taboos, limitations, differences, bans, responsibilities, charges, classes, chiefs, royal persons, gods, Jesus Christ from the Cross. Items of clothing can also be *snyat*: for example Lenin, translating Engels, writes of the *snyatie* of the fig leaf of absolutism.[8] In all this, the *snyatie* presupposes the downward transfer of something from its lofty or fixed position and an ensuing dramatic change in its state: the crops from the fields, a picture from the wall, a minister from his post, a death mask from a face, things into a concept (now this is Hegelian: Lenin writes about the *snyatie* of a mask to illustrate the making of a concept)[9] or onto a film (you shoot a film in English but *snyat'* is what you do to it in Russian), and so on up to the point where, not without logic and, I assume, not without the *aufgehoben* memory of the long hegelization of the Russian word, we find *snyatie* in contemporary Russian slang as indicating the discharge and relief of sexual tension.

The notes and references to Hegel in the writings of Lenin, the enfant terrible of the Russian blend of science and revolution, never put into question the notion of *Aufhebung* and its translation as *snyatie*, although they do involve plans as to how to correct and extract the "rational kernel" of Hegel's dialectic from its idealistic captivity. The rational kernel included the unity and coincidence of opposites and contradictions in concepts but also in material reality, the uninhibited passage of one opposite into the other (for example, the possibility for the singular to be universal and vice versa), the simultaneity of cancellation and preservation, including the cancellation and preservation of a thing in its concept, the movement, ultimately, of a destruction that conserves whatever it destroys by a sort of stenography. Lenin was especially fascinated by the curve as opposed to the straight line: The curve was part of a vortex, whose endless upward movement expressed the true nature of progression as preservation through destruction. What still needed to be done to set things right with dialectical progression was to follow Marx's prescription and reverse Hegel's idealism by putting it properly on its feet. For Lenin, this reversal, like the *snyatie* itself, implied a downward movement. "Down with Heaven: materialism" was Lenin's concise description of what Hegel's system needed.[10] The upward movement of the vortex, the movement that preserved what it destroyed and destroyed what it preserved, was hence seen as accomplished through taking what was up (heaven, god, absolute spirit, ideas, but also the tsar, the bourgeoisie . . .) down: No wonder the translation of *Aufhebung* as *snyatie* weathered the ordeals of revolution and the decades that followed as the very epitome of indestructibility in destruction. It is as if the issue of translation became inscribed and thus vanished into the radicalism of the revolutionary act. In truth it was *snyat.*

AUFHEBUNG WITH A *DIFFÉRANCE*

In sharp contrast to the early and widespread Russian acceptance of Hegel's term in a single definitive translation, for many decades now, in the context of French theoretical thinking, the translation of *aufheben* has been a problem engendering heated discussions and controversies. Indeed, in a late text he presented at a translators' conference, Derrida even turned these discussions and his own "relevant" translation of the term—in French, this relevant translation is, indeed, *relever*—into a parable of translation per se.[11] Can and should this term, this so very German term, be translated at all? The temptation to let it stand, so to say, in its Ur-form is always there, whatever Hegel might have thought about it. Or should one look for a proper "citizen of the French language" in compliance with Hegel's belief that science should employ the resources of the respective natural language? And, since there seems to be no natural equivalent of Hegel's term in French, should one invent a neologism as a sort of compromise between keeping the German word and adapting an existing word? In the course of answering such questions, suggestions proliferated: *supprimer, abroger, enlever, assumer, sublimer, surprimer, relever, sursumer* . . . [12]

This series of suggestions is bound up with a strong conviction that the very understanding of Hegel is at stake here. According to Nancy, who dedicated a whole book to the term, commenting on the *Aufhebung* is very much "the program for a general (and perhaps absolute) commentary of Hegel," and, he adds in a footnote, "every great study of Hegel is, in effect, a study of the *Aufhebung*, and for good reason."[13] Several decades earlier, Alexandre Kojève, a Russian philosopher who played quite a role in the spread of Hegelian studies in France, observed that "one could say that Hegelian dialectic is summarized by one single fundamental category, the category of dialectical suppression (*Aufheben*)."[14] And, in a text dedicated to the role in the spread of Hegelian studies in France of yet another Russian philosopher, Alexandre Koyré, Jean Wahl asked: "How should one translate *Aufheben*? This is the key to Hegelianism."[15]

Jean Wahl thought *Aufheben* as the key to Hegelianism was especially difficult for the French, "if it were possible to speak of differences based on nationality." By way of answering all of Jean Wahl's concerns at once—concerns about the key to Hegel's philosophy but also concerns about translation and the French difference—Derrida's major (non)concept *différance* is offered as a "translation" of the difference between two types of difference in Hegel. This difference struck Derrida while reading a text where Koyré proposes the translation, in French, of long citations from Hegel's *Jena Logic*. *Différance*, hence, is the translation of a difference between Hegelian differences, a micrological difference, as Derrida would later describe it, about which Hegel remains silent but which Derrida detects via Koyré and for which Hegel and Koyré do not but Derrida does offer a term.[16] Thus, as Derrida himself tells the story in *Positions*, *différance* appears as the outcome of his effort to differentiate his own conception of difference from what he sees as Hegel's reduction of difference to a contradiction that can be resolved, internalized, canceled, and—could we say it at this point?—*snyat'*. *Différance*, Derrida goes on to specify, marks the point of greatest, indeed "almost absolute" proximity to Hegel, in order to, at this very point, break away from the system of speculative dialectics by writing the double sense of the *Aufhebung* in another way.[17] As a result of this procedure, *différance* presents its own francophone (*sic!*) challenge to philosophical translatability. By becoming the simultaneous inscription of the phonic and the silent, the differentiated in space and the deferred in time, *différance* emerges as the quite untranslatable French naming of the very difference from and deferral of the untranslatable *Aufhebung*. Returning to Nancy's observation about Hegel, at this point we might say that commenting on *différance*'s differing from and deferring of the *Aufhebung* may provide the program for a general commentary of deconstruction.

In the framework of the tireless differing and deferring, which involves *différance* but also other of Derrida's (non)concepts, Derrida proposes his own French translation of *aufheben*. This translation is *relever*. Like the German *aufheben* and the Russian *snyat'*, *relever*, we will hardly be surprised, is a polysemous word. There is, furthermore, a shift of meaning between the verb *relever* and the noun *relève*, which means relief (there is a crossing point here with the Russian *snyatie* as the *snyatie* of tension) as well as—Derrida and Nancy are especially emphatic about this—a changing of the guard. The basic meanings of the verb *relever*, however, are to stand up, pick up, pull up, raise, roll up, lift up . . . The mystery that concerns me now becomes apparent. Among its various meanings, *aufheben* does include the meanings of raise and lift up. There is no doubt, furthermore, that the Hegelian system outlines a relentless upward movement. Nevertheless, so far as *aufheben* is concerned, Hegel insists that its remarkable quality, displaying the speculative genius of the German language, consists in encompassing the two meanings of cancel and conserve and *not* move up or down. And yet, down it goes to the East of Germany and up to the West of it.

THE *SNYATIE RELEVÉ*

It should be noted at this point that the tendency to introduce an upward verticality in the rendering of *aufheben* is not confined to the French and to Derrida's translation. In English, it was introduced as early as 1865 through the now widely accepted rendering of Hegel's term as *sublate* and *sublation. Sublation* is derivative of the Latin *tollere,* which has the double meaning of raise up and destroy, thus functioning as a sort of photographic negative to the Russian *snyat'*. It should be noted that Hegel had explicit reservations about the applicability of *tollere* in this case. Nevertheless and in spite of alternative translations, *sublation* has prevailed in English philosophical literature and has probably enhanced in its turn the idea that Hegel's term embraces an upward movement. This idea tends to surface in a variety of contexts, sometimes accompanied by an acknowledgment of the fact that Hegel is not interested in this meaning, sometimes not. Thus, in *A Hegel Dictionary* Michael Inwood claims that "despite Hegel's silence on the matter, it is reasonable to see sense (1) [of *Aufhebung*], 'elevation,' as an ingredient in its Hegelian meaning."[18] Alan Bass's note in his translation of Derrida's "Différance" betrays no awareness of Hegel's silence on the matter when he explains that

> *Aufhebung* literary means "lifting up"; but it also contains the double meaning of conservation and negation. For Hegel, dialectics is a process of *Aufhebung*: every concept is to be negated and lifted up to a higher sphere in which it is thereby conserved.[19]

Thus, in Bass's gloss, lifting up is the stipulation that can explain how a thing can be simultaneously negated and conserved.

Going back to the French story, we can see that, with Nancy, the awareness of and the simultaneous disregard for Hegel's silence on the matter of elevation takes the form of a division in his own text. On the one hand, in a long footnote, Nancy offers an account of the instances in which Hegel comments on the term—an account that cannot but demonstrate the absence of any up or down considerations. On the other hand, in the corpus of his text, Nancy justifies Derrida's translation of *aufheben* as *relever*, that is, as elevate. The justification, notably, involves a critique of the prevalent French translation as *supprimer. Supprimer* means cancel, remove, abolish but it also means to suppress or knock down. It comes from the Latin *supprimo* which also has the additional meanings of sinking or sending to the bottom. Although the credit for the spreading of this translation in French literature has been attributed to Jean Hyppolite,[20] it was used before that.[21] Alexandre Koyré resorts sometimes to *surmonter*[22] (to rise above, surmount, overcome) or to *suppression*,[23] but in the majority of cases he uses *supprimer* and, in a 1931 text dealing with the intrinsic untranslatability of Hegel, he glosses Hegel's term as "le fameux *Aufheben* voulant dire en même temps supprimer et conserver" ("the famous *Aufheben,* meaning simultaneously to suppress/destroy and to conserve").[24] *Supprimer* is the translation used throughout the 1933–39 lectures on Hegel by Alexandre Kojève, who would also occasionally render the term as "dialectical suppression." Like the Russian *snyat'*, therefore, *supprimer* involves notions of downward movement and, in Koyré's and Kojève's usage, which tends to displace "destroy and conserve" with "suppress and conserve," it appears to be the translation of *snyat'* qua translation of *aufheben.* "I speak Russian in fifteen languages"—said another influential Russian of this period, the polyglot structuralist Roman Jakobson. So far as *aufheben* is concerned, Koyré and Kojève seem to be speaking Russian in German and French.

Kojève is, indeed, careful to note that *supprimer dialectiquement*, to abolish or suppress in a dialectical way, means to abolish/suppress (*supprimer*) while conserving the abolished/suppressed (*supprimé*), which is "sublimated (*sublimé*) in and by this suppression. . . . The abolished/suppressed (*supprimé*) entity . . . is sublimated (*sublimée*) or elevated (*élevée*) in a more comprehensive mode of being."[25] Or, as Derrida would put it decades later in his account of how he came to his own translation of the term, Hegel's major word means "to abolish/suppress and elevate at the same time" ("*à la fois supprimer et élever*").[26]

If *aufheben* means to suppress *and* elevate—although, let me say it one last time, Hegel was explicitly concerned with the simultaneity of destruction and preservation rather than with the simultaneity of up and down movements—the question is why in certain cases (Hyppolite, Kojève, the habitual Russian translation) the simultaneity of destruction and preservation would appear as taking down while in other cases (Derrida, the habitual English translation) the upward movement would be seen as better fitting the selfsame simultaneity? In fact, a decade before Derrida suggested *relever*, *supprimer* is conspicuously absent in a crucial context where Lacan refers to the *Aufhebung*. Lacan, as it is well known, was among the most ardent listeners of Kojève, whom he recognized as his only "master for having introduced [him] to Hegel."[27] Notwithstanding the controversies surrounding the nature and the degree of Kojève's influence, the connection between some of Lacan's key terms such as desire and jouissance and Kojève's reading of Hegel cannot be doubted. To add a further twist to the translation romance, the text I am referring to—*La signification du phallus, Die Bedeutung des Phallus*—was initially presented in German at the Max Planck Institute in Munich in 1958. In the French version of the text—curiously, it is claimed that it offers "without modification, *sans modification*" the original German presentation as if the translation into French is not a modification—Hegel's term is introduced twice in German in order to describe the phallus as

> the sign of the latency with which everything signifiable is struck as soon as it is raised (*aufgehoben*) to the function of signifier.
>
> The phallus is the signifier of this *Aufhebung* itself which it inaugurates (initiates) by its own disappearance.[28]

Notably, in this passage, which echoes Kojève's description of "dialectical suppression," *aufgehoben* is used to render only the raising part of the process. It would appear, consequently, that with the simultaneity of destruction and preservation of the *Aufhebung* there is a changing of the guard—if we are allowed to anticipate Derrida at this precise point—from its mode *supprimé* into an elevating mode when the Phallus becomes its signifier. Since it is the function of the Phallus to ensure sexual difference and preclude the "dream of the philosophers" of turning two into one—as Lacan would much later, yet still led by concerns with sexual difference, refer to the *Aufhebung*[29]—the unacceptability of the downward direction of *supprimer*, so seamlessly translating the Russian revolutionary *snyatie*, would seem to be ensuing from this phallic exigency. Up it must go! Thus, while with Lenin's "down with Heaven," there seems to surface the connection between the *Aufhebung* qua *snyatie* and the Bolshevik revolution, the raising of the *Aufhebung* into the Phallus, to which Derrida's *différance* will then try to counter the *encore encore!* of differing and deferring, becomes the symptom of the gender troubles of the twentieth century.

THE ANTINOMIES OF SEXUAL DIFFERENCE

The two directions that the translation of the *Aufhebung* take thus seem to embrace the two sides of dialectics as discussed by Alain Badiou in his *Theory of the Subject*: the "strong" and the "weak" side, side of forces and side of places, historical side and structural side, topological and algebraic, one under the sign of destruction and the other one under the sign of lack. Structural dialectics privileges "weak differences" at the expense of strong differences. It reduces difference to the gap between positions. It prefers the correlations of pure exclusion, of positional scission, and of interchangeability to what, under the name of "struggle of opposites," is trying to apprehend destruction as a quality of force. It fixes opposites in a symmetry or in an invariable dissymmetry instead of grasping the principal becoming of the secondary. It encounters the real as an obstacle. . . . The strong side of dialectics, in contrast, the side of force, involves destruction as the lack of lack, as an excess of the real.

Between Lacan and mathematics, Badiou reenvisions the dialectical vortex by terming this moment of dialectics *torsion.* Torsion is destruction that—and this, Badiou notes, is its dialectical status—puts an end to repetition while positioning the innovative rupture into a circular flexion. Revolution and what Badiou would later elaborate in his theory of the event as the eruption of the new would thus belong to this side of dialectics.

Badiou's understanding of dialectics according to which torsion is "this moment of interruption that makes lack stray into destruction"[30] allows us, consequently, to discern in sexual difference the contraption that makes destruction stray into lack, a straying exemplified by the translation of the *Aufhebung* now down now up from revolution to sexual difference. Not only does sexual difference appear to be, as has justly been observed, a structural fatality but, distributed by the phallus as the signifier of lack, it emerges as the very machine that ushers the dialectics of forces into structural dialectics, keeping lack in place, warding off the lack of lack, blocking torsion. Not only is sexual difference constitutively immune to revolution, it is the antirevolutionary immunity system per se.

And yet, there is another side to it, another side that is the very same side, insofar as the Moebius strip is Lacan's reference at this point. It is notoriously known that Lenin's definition of a revolutionary situation (which the velvet revolutions in Eastern Europe, in fact, confirmed) took a somewhat obscene turn when he described it as the situation where "those below do not want to and those above are not able to."[31] For Lenin, it was important to emphasize that it was not enough for those below not to want, it was necessary that those above couldn't [rule] in the old way. With the revolutionary situation taking the form of a two-sided sexual malfunction, Lacan's dictum "there is no sexual relation" turns sexual difference into a permanent revolution.

It would appear consequently that:

Sexual difference belongs to the weak differences of structural dialectics.

Sexual difference belongs to the strong differences of the dialectics of force.
Sexual difference is the jamming of torsion and hence a device of the status quo.
Sexual difference is perpetual torsion and hence the matrix of revolution.

It is no wonder, therefore, that feminism, by necessity grappling with the antinomies of sexual difference, has—with reference once again to Joan Scott's analysis of the discursive impasses in the history of women's movements—"nothing but paradoxes to offer." No wonder, too, that the age of feminism is contemporaneous with the age of revolutions. As the simultaneous reservoir and paralysis of destruction qua torsion and hence of the new, sexual difference is inescapably implicated in projects to promote or arrest change. And while efforts to forestall the new unavoidably involve attempts to freeze sexual identities, its promotion has a variety of options—a variety of ways to get trapped in the antinomies, one might say. The wavering, which I discussed in the first chapter, of convoluted institutionalized tampering with sex and sexual identities in the former communist countries offers a sometimes dramatic, sometimes comic illustration of this state of affairs: between the radical projects for doing away with sex during the revolutionary stages, the more or less conscious relapse to traditional ideas of difference during the consolidation of the regimes, and the laissez-faire of the late years of the regime's erosion when all this coexisted in a seething nonreflective mixture . . . These developments mirrored—with all the complications of mirroring that the story of the *Aufhebung* already suggests—developments in Western feminism, which remained caught up in the same antinomies, now relying on difference for its revolutionary potential, now trying to unmask it as the agent of normalization.

The problem acquires its most acute articulation with the appearance of Judith Butler's *Gender Trouble*, which transforms the field of the debate by introducing performativity as a concept that exposes the propensity of sexual difference to serve as a mechanism blocking change.[32] Performativity—Butler restates in her next book in the face of the frequent misunderstanding that accompanied the wide acclaim for this term—

> cannot be understood outside of a process of iterability, a regularized and constrained repetition of norms. . . . "Performance" is not a singular "act" or event, but a ritualized production, a ritual reiterated under and through constraint, under and through the force of prohibition and taboo, with the threat of ostracism and even death controlling and compelling the shape of the production, but not, I still insist, determining it fully in advance.[33]

And so, gender is the not always efficient reiteration of constraining, painful, and sometimes even deadly norms. The question, accordingly, is—and Butler continues to work out the implications of this question in her subsequent work—how to conceive of constraint and repetition themselves as self-defeating and hence subversive. No matter what the solution is, however, sexual difference per se is a normative device arresting transformation and change. As such, it deserves little sympathy. Butler's concern with "doing" and "undoing" gender, with performing and nonperforming sexual identities is ultimately a concern with sabotaging sexual difference tout court.

Joan Copjec's response to *Gender Trouble* in her essay "Sex and the Euthanasia of Reason" shifts precisely this premise. Copjec challenges some of Butler's "fundamental assumptions on the ground that they may not support the political goals the book wants to defend,"[34] thus claiming that Butler's political goals would be better supported through Copjec's own position, that is, through the theoretical investment in a sexual difference that "does not budge." Via a Kantian reading of Lacan's formulas of sexuation, Copjec aligns Lacan's formula of femininity with Kant's mathematical antinomy and Lacan's formula of masculinity with Kant's dynamical antinomy. This argument takes Copjec ultimately to a discussion of the superego where it is stated that

> the prohibition proper to the superego renders something unsayable and undoable, to be sure, but it does not say what we should not say or do; it merely imposes a limit that makes everything we do and say seem as nought compared to what we cannot.[35]

The whole drama of the limit and the abjected beings created through this limit, which animates Butler's concern, the drama, that is, of the reiterative doing and undoing of the limit, is hence reduced to a trivial aspect of the prohibition proper to the superego. This also amounts to saying that this drama and hence Butler's theoretical optics focusing on the effects of the limit belong to the masculine side of the equation. Instead, Copjec's wager is with "an ethics of inclusion and of the unlimited, that is, an ethics proper to the woman."[36] In Copjec's view, therefore, Butler's political goals, her concern with the abjected and the excluded, can have their hope precisely in a sexual difference that does not budge. Sexual difference is the proper machine for transformation.

EIRON AND *ALAZON*

Although sexual difference does not budge, sexual identity is nonetheless fraudulent—at this point Copjec is in agreement with Butler. Sex is the real where language fails; masculinity and femininity simply qualify the failure. There is the masculine and the feminine side to this failure, the way there is, with Kant, a dynamical and a mathematical side to the failure of pure reason. Hence, although sexual difference is real, every claim to positive sexual identity is a sham. In fact, if there are two distinctive types of failure, there are also two distinctive types of fraudulence. "All pretensions of masculinity are, then, sheer imposture, just as every display of femininity is sheer masquerade."[37]

Copjec's two types of gender fraudulence evoke the dramatis personae of ancient comedy with masculinity as the *alazon* and femininity as the *eiron*. The *alazon* is, precisely, an impostor. A boasting soldier, a braggart, a miser, an irritable and despotic military and paternal figure who wants to control everybody else through his money and social power: The *alazon* imagines that he is bigger than he is and that he knows what, in fact, he does not know. His role is to hinder and block the other characters. In the comedy of sexual difference, we might say the *alazon* is the side that pretends to know what sexual difference is. The *eiron*, in contrast, is the master of self-deprecatory understatement. He undermines the impostures of the *alazon* by masquerading as being lesser than he is. He appears to be smaller than he is, and he appears to know less than he knows—it is precisely this state of affairs that Joan Rivière describes in the article claiming that femininity is masquerade, which Lacan valued so highly.[38] It is this superior knowledge masquerading as ignorance that helps him overthrow the *alazon* and liberate the other characters. Once again, we might say that the *eiron* is that side of sexual difference that pretends not to know that which cannot be known.

Out of the figure of the *eiron*, Aristotle develops the idea of irony. Hegel, however, is the one who associates womankind with the "everlasting irony of the community." Badiou, in turn, connects Hegel's statement to Lacan's formula of femininity, read by him as "woman inexists in the whole."[39] Now, if we would try to imagine gender theory from the point of view of this inexistence in the whole, the point of view of the *eiron*, of the one who unsettles—if I am allowed this turn of phrase at this precise moment—the transitional *alazony* of the community, what would such a theory look like? Wouldn't the *eiron* try to thwart the *alazon*'s posturing as the one who knows what sexual difference is? Wouldn't Butler's program for the doing and undoing of gender come as close as can be to the *eironic* stance? Wouldn't we have to admit that this is the theory, always concerned with the excluded as it is, that could answer Copjec's call for an ethics proper to the woman—an ethics of inclusion and of the unlimited, an ethics, consequently, of misericordia toward the abjected and the constitutively left out?

This means that the sexual difference that does not budge encompasses the difference between its alazonic imposture and its eironic undoing; it also amounts to saying that the theory criticized by Copjec is also the theory that her own conceptualization of sexual difference calls for.

IRONY AND REVOLUTION

Initially I meant this *Aufhebung* story to be comic. In the summer of 2001, I was in Vienna, at the Institute for the Human Sciences. There I was asked to give a talk about gender in the former Soviet bloc countries. At the time, I was expected to be an expert on this topic, but it was a painful topic for me, the topic of a personal but also, I thought, a historical failure, a muteness, an amnesia, an unnamable loss. Hannah Arendt thought that this affliction, this impossibility to name the loss, which she discerned in the postwar melancholia of the French Resistance, was an aspect of any postrevolutionary situation. As Wendy Brown has put it, "What kind of lost object is this?"[40] Talking about this mysterious lost object seemed to me like talking about Hannah Arendt's unicorns and fairy queens—not in terms of something that had existed but in terms of something that might have been. It is this "might have been" that no longer could be recalled. Perhaps, there never ever had been anything worth recalling. I knew that I was unable to give such a talk. Nevertheless, I had to keep trying. Between the Scylla and Charybdis of autism and convertibility I had to find a way to name the thing that could not be named.

And yet, there was something comic about my dumbness. There was something intrinsically funny about the uncontrollable inversions in the terms and the situations, which I described as heterotopian homonymy. The split, the reduplication, which heterotopian homonymy introduced into the language that had to be used in all seriousness, resembled too much the mechanism of comedy: Whether one was aware or not, an *eiron* or an *alazon*, statements unavoidably meant something more and something else than intended. It is no wonder that a unique blend of precision and humor became the brand name for the Ljubljana Lacanian School, which has proved that laughter and thinking are twins as no one else has done so far: Not so much the geographical but rather the (former) political position of Slovenia between two "topoi" (and also, perhaps, as Alenka Zupančič tells us in *The Shortest Shadow*, the existence of single, plural, *and* dual number in Slovenian grammar) seems to have allowed a sustained philosophical mastery of reduplicating discourses and visions. As Žižek's theoretical recapitulation in the *Parallax View* demonstrates, the very "*parallax gap*, the confrontation of two closely linked perspectives between which no neutral common ground is possible,"[41] reveals the subversive core of dialectics.

That summer in Vienna, stirring up forgotten languages and memories and stumbling on the way in which Russian thought had the *Aufhebung* taken down in the Revolution and how Lacan had it *aufgehoben* into the Phallus, I was struck by the pertinence of the *Aufhebung* as an example of the inversion and contestation characterizing heterotopian homonymy. Here it was, the unfathomable German term, standing in its Ur-form in the middle of Europe. Up the phallic signifier goes to the West of it and down to the East of it. This inversion seemed to fit into the empirical reversals of the vicissitudes of women's issues in the Cold War heterotopia: from below, through grassroots feminist movements in the West and from above, through the postrevolutionary bureaucracy in the Eastern bloc countries, and then the other way round. What better way to speak about the dramas of gender than the up and down fortunes of the *Aufhebung*? In view of my early and relentless indoctrination that the best way to negate and yet preserve something is through its being taken down, the inverted destinies of the *Aufhebung* struck me as so funny that I spent a couple of weeks laughing, looking on the Internet for pictures of the highest skyscrapers in New York and the deepest metro stations in Moscow. I was still doing this when somebody called me and asked me whether I was watching TV. No, I said. Well, you should, they said. And this is how I saw the New York towers go down.

Up to that point my "comic" plan had been to use the *Aufhebung* as an entrance to Seyla Benhabib's claim that "what women can do today is restore irony to the dialectic, by defeating the pompous march of historical necessity."[42] When the *snyatie* of the *relève* took such a literal shape, however, it revealed me to be the object rather than the cunning East European subject of the irony. Instead of transforming my theoretical autism into the knowing stance of the *eiron*, I, it turned out, like the *alazon*, had been wearing—with a reference to Alenka Zupančič's discussion of comedy[43]—the real outside myself. Although I was unaware of it, the *Aufhebung* had opened its apocalyptic potential, pointing toward, to put it in Badiou's terms, the other side of the dialectic, the one of "destruction, of the more-than-real, of force."[44]

Recently, Giorgio Agamben has added another angle to this story by calling attention to the possibility that the double sense of *aufheben*, so much admired by Hegel, may have been the inheritance of Martin Luther's translation as *aufheben* of Saint Paul's antinomic usage of the Greek word *katargein* ("to cancel, destroy, render inoperative," i.e., as in Saint Paul, to destroy the law by faith is to preserve it).[45] This sweeping perspective—which is already alluded to at the end of Derrida's text on translation where Martin Luther appears as the arch-translator—turns the transmigration of the *Aufhebung* from one translation onto another into the trajectory of an excess of the real that makes it impossible to avoid the problem of destruction.

In short, something more and something better than the heterotopian foreclosure of utopia might be at stake in cases like that of *Aufhebung*. The terminological parallax—comic or uncanny, as the case may be—might be the carrier of the lightning of the real. It is noteworthy that at the beginning of the momentous 1980s Merab Mamardashvili questions—talking not of Hegel but of Kant—the Russian translation as *snyatie*. To translate *aufheben* as *snyat'*, he comments, implies taking knowledge down in order to open space for faith. Translating it as "raising up," however, would amount to "taking it up in front of my eyes in order to see it, to examine it" and thus "open a place in the world for myself with my actions and my thinking."[46] Mamardashvili's suggestion for a reversal in the translation is thus inscribed in the anthropology that subtends the political agenda of the last decade of communism and that will concern us in the next chapter.

And yet, will it be just chance that a rendering of the *Aufhebung* as falling has made its reappearance in French? Catherine Malabou, whose "transformation" of the *Aufhebung* into "plasticity" as "sculpture" and "explosion" opens a new chapter in its vicissitudes, notes that "if the sublation (*relève*) can sublate itself, it is precisely because it ends by *seeing itself* and can consequently *let (itself) fall* [(se) laisser tomber]."[47]

Whatever else the uncanny plasticity of the *Aufhebung* proclaims, it certainly means the irrecoverable obsoleteness of the lost fairy queens and unicorns of the "velvet" East European revolutions. As revolutions, they have failed. Their "autistic" message, if there ever was one, evaporated before it materialized. Was this message, the perhaps impossible message a message about revolution without destruction? And has this not been the impossible message of feminism? And is not the impossibility a manner of retaining, after all? The bifurcating history of the translations of the *Aufhebung*, it seems to me, is one of those vanishing traces where the mystery still lingers.

CHAPTER FOUR

An Unfinished Project: Man as Comedy

Gaius Baltar: Then who—or what—are you?
"Head" Six: I am an angel of god sent here to guide you, to protect you, and to love you.
Gaius Baltar: To what end?
"Head" Six: To the end of the human race.

—*Battlestar Galactica*

References to Simone de Beauvoir's celebrated first sentence of the second book of *The Second Sex*—"One is not born, but rather becomes, a woman"[1]—frequently ignore the claim Beauvoir makes earlier on that "woman is not a completed entity, but rather a becoming."[2] Beauvoir's point in emphasizing woman as becoming is thus not reducible to the problematic of forced identities but presupposes, rather, that woman, like man, is not completed or fixed: Man, Beauvoir notes with reference to Merleau-Ponty, is a "historical idea" and because of this also a project and a task. One becomes a woman, but one also becomes a man. One becomes a man in the sense of "human male"; one also becomes a man in the sense of "human being." One is not born a man; one is not born a woman; and one is not born, but rather becomes, a human being.

It is in this third sense that the word "man" appears in a short talk delivered in French by Merab Mamardashvili at a conference in Paris, in 1988, that is, on the eve of the political changes in Eastern Europe. In this talk, titled "The European Responsibility," Mamardashvili also conjures up the idea of man as a project. "There is an organ of life, specific to man; this organ is history"—he states in stark contrast to the "end of history" debate that would mark the epoch. "Man is always in process of becoming, and each history can be defined as the history of his effort to become a man. Man does not exist—man is becoming."[3]

Thus at a critical political juncture for Eastern Europe Mamardashvili evokes the selfsame idea of man as a task and a project, as an unfinished creation, that sustains Beauvoir's argument at the inception of the most decisive decades in the history of feminism. Whereas Beauvoir refers to man in order to claim the right to becoming for woman, Mamardashvili connects this idea to (Western) Europe[4] in order to take a stand for the impending changes in Eastern Europe. There is, however, a noticeable shift. Although the point, for Simone de Beauvoir, is to claim for woman the projectivity that distinguishes "man" and that an inconsistent universality tacitly denies her, she has no doubts regarding the standing of the idea per se, the idea, that is, of man as an undefined and unfinished creature, as his own open-ended undertaking. For Mamardashvili, in contrast, the problem is that, at the moment when Eastern Europe is emerging from decades of arrested change, man's projectivity itself seems to have been compromised, because of, as he puts it, "fatigue with the tough historical work sustaining the effort."[5]

"You Europeans . . . have stopped thinking about what the essence of your existence is. You no longer possess the keen awareness that the human being is in the first place a constant effort to become a human being, and that this is not a natural state but a state that is continually created."[6] And he goes on to outline how he, the Georgian outsider, inherited this awareness from Cartesian philosophy, from the Renaissance that made us "irreversibly modern," from the Gospels, from the Greco-Roman world. "But a fatigue and a forgetfulness of one's beginnings might set in. Herein lies the danger for Europe."

Mamardashvili's fear is that man is no longer becoming. Somehow he has become finished. Between the end of the forties and the end of the eighties—at the time when the *Aufhebung*, as discussed in the previous chapter, with its "changing of the guard" to become the marker of gender trouble—something happened that rendered the project of man inoperative. In his book dedicated to the twentieth century Alain Badiou poses this mystery at the center of his concern, observing that the twentieth century began under the sign of a particularly radical project for the transformation of the human being and that this project, or rather, the projectivity itself, the idea that man is his own unfinished task, has paradoxically vanished precisely at a time when technological means for such transformations seem to be more than ever at hand. For Badiou, this is a symptom of the blindness of the appropriation of technology by economics, of the fact that "science—therein lies its grandeur—possesses problems; it does not have a project." It would seem that, between Beauvoir and Mamardashvili, a "revenge of the scientific problem over the political project" came to pass.

> Believe me, inane ethical committees will never provide us with an answer to the following question: "What is to be done about this fact: that science knows how to make a new man?' " And since there is no project, or as long as there is no project, everyone knows there is only one answer: profit will tell us what to do.[7]

FATIGUE

About a decade after Mamardashvili's death Giorgio Agamben sums up various aspects of Mamardashvili's fears in terms of the idling of the "anthropological machine."[8] The anthropological machine is a device that produces humanity through the incessant articulation of the separation between man and animal, a separation that passes first and foremost within man.

In himself, man has no nature of his own, no identity, no "rank" (as Agamben asserts with reference to Renaissance thinker Pico della Mirandola's *Oration*, wrongly rendered, Agamben points out, as *Oration on the Dignity of Man*). The fundamental procedure, which ensures the becoming human of the living being and the transformation of animal nature into human history, is provided by metaphysics, which, consequently, is not an innocuous academic pastime but the very mechanism of the anthropological machine. Agamben thus endorses the view according to which man is the product of a metaphysical operation and, as Gilbert Simondon more starkly puts it, the invention of Socrates, who, "by emphasizing man's radical distance from everything that is nature, founded humanism on the 'anthropological difference.' "[9]

The work of the anthropological machine is not an event that has been accomplished once and for all. It has to be constantly renewed. Because of the manner in which it works, however, that is, by the suspension and capture of animal life, the machine opens up a space of exception, a zone that is perfectly empty and where what is obtained through constant rearticulation is neither animal nor human life, but "only a life that is separated and excluded from itself—only a *bare* life."[10] In this book, Agamben's most pertinent example of the bare life is the tick whose existence is totaled by the drop of blood. The drop of blood is all the tick needs to fulfill itself, and yet, it turns out, it could forgo it for years, emptied even of this minimal characteristic.

Today, Agamben argues, the anthropological machine is inoperative. In agreement with the Hegelian-Kojevan idea of the end of history, man has reached his historical *telos*: The traditional modes for the production of man—poetry, religion, philosophy—have been transformed into cultural spectacle and private experience and have lost their historical efficacy. The only task that seems to have retained some seriousness is the management of biological life, that is, of the very animality of man: Humanity takes on its own physiology as its ultimate directive, exposing the fact that from the start politics has been biopolitics. The result is total depoliticization, a humanity about which it is hard to say whether it is still human, a life that can no longer be recognized as human or animal. "The total humanization of the animal coincides with the total animalization of man."[11] Or, to put it in the words of one of the more cheerful accounts of this state of affairs, we have put an end to the Cartesian preposterousness of the "human exception."[12]

Agamben suggests three further scenarios pertaining to this situation. Two of them are sketched from Heidegger's perspective. Man either (1) seeks to take on his own animality and govern it by means of technology, or (2) as the "shepherd of being," he neither lets his animality remain hidden nor makes it an object of mastery, but thinks it as such, as pure abandonment. The third scenario is unfolded out of Benjamin's concept of the "saved night" and is illustrated via a late work by Titian, depicting the "workless" side-by-side remoteness between a nymph and a shepherd.

> In their fulfillment, the lovers who have lost their mystery contemplate a human nature rendered perfectly inoperative—the inactivity [*inoperasità*] and *desoeuvrement* of the human and the animal as the supreme and unsavable figure of life.[13]

Inoperativeness, "standstill," "desoeuvrement," postcoital neutralization, "suspension of the suspension" are the terms that describe the idling of the anthropogenetic machine. Set against Mamardashvili's preoccupation with effort, tough historical work, continual creation, and change, Agamben's perspective might offer "man" as the ultimate example of the heterotopian homonymy that marked the post–Cold War decade.

MAN IS IMPOSSIBLE BUT HE HAPPENS

It could be argued that Agamben *restores* the animal to Heidegger's open.[14] With Mamardashvili, the unnaturalness of man is taken for granted. Hence, although Mamardashvili never tires of emphasizing the "unnaturalness" of man and his difference from the animal, he does not really see him as the product of differentiation from the animal. With Mamardashvili, man is the offspring of a complete break, of an unforeseeable and unpredictable ontological interruption. The interruption occurs as an act of thought, which takes place in the void (its logic and laws occur only retroactively, *at the second step*) and which changes the world irreversibly. Such an act effecting transformation and change he defines as an event.[15]

In an article that Mamardashvili's publisher Y. P. Senokosov read in manuscript in 1978 and which appeared postmortem as an appendix to his 1970s manuscript *The Arrow of Knowledge*, Mamardashvili expounds this idea with regard to science (which, with him, provides a paradigmatic framework for the way an event functions).

> Through the very act of its accomplishment [new] knowledge is inscribed in science *qua* comprehension of things, in science's semantic and logical orders, but *as an event or free change* it is non-deductible and unpredictable, i.e. it cannot be arrived at through the uninterrupted continuation of the preceding ordering of the states of understanding (and if yes, it is possible only *post factum*, in a reverse analytical actualization).[16]

Being an ontological break, the act of thought is subjectless—it happens at the level of the nothing-man (Nichto-chelovek). Man is "born" at the second step. Like the act of thought whose aftermath he is, man is a retroactive occurrence. Man is impossible, but he happens.[17]

WRITTEN OR ORAL: ONE LAST GLANCE

So where does the effort, the tough work, the responsibility belong? Man, it turns out, *is* effort, tough work, responsibility; and yet he is the product of an acephalous, unforeseeable, and unmerited event, a question of grace. Before proceeding with these queries, a detour seems necessary, which concerns an unresolved issue about Mamardashvili's work. This detour will take us one last time to the problem with which this book began: the problem of orality, of living and thinking in the *phonē*. Much of Mamardashvili's oeuvre was published after his death (in fact, it keeps appearing), and much of it was oral to begin with. As I already pointed out, in the 1980s seminar epoch, Mamardashvili exemplified the virtues of orality. Along with the publication of his series of lectures and other oral performances, however, new, heretofore unpublished manuscripts have also appeared, tilting the balance toward the writing. Today, his Bulgarian commentator, philosopher Deyan Deyanov, judges Mamardashvili's reputation as a man "not of the written word" to be the result of erroneously reading the predominantly written Mamardashvili of the 1970s via the predominantly spoken Mamardasvhili of the 1980s. Deyanov reassesses his own earlier conviction that Mamardashvili created not a spoken philosophy that could be written down but a spoken philosophy as opposed to the written one, and claims that this view cannot do justice to the really innovative ideas that Mamardashvili conveyed both in his publications during his lifetime and in the manuscripts that appeared after his death. Deyanov thus seems to draw a line between the earlier written oeuvre and the later predominantly oral production (lectures, conference presentations, interviews), placing now the emphasis on the written pieces as the truly important part of Mamardashvili's work.[18]

There are, to be sure, significant differences between Mamardashvili's written and oral output. His written work tends to be immensely dense and difficult; his series of lectures and other oral presentations, on the contrary, tend to be accessible and seductive. Mamardashvili was keenly aware of his audiences, and there is no doubt that the opaqueness of his writing was at least partially a stratagem to deal with censorship. The story of his unfinished treatise *The Arrow of Knowledge*,[19] which appeared after Mamardashvili's death, is typical. Its initial title was "A Sketch of the Natural History of Gnoseology: Toward a Treatise on the Development of Knowledge," and it was written in the 1970s at a time when the philosopher worked at the Institute for the History of Natural Science and Technology. There is a whole mute story of continual academic displacement behind this appointment. Whatever unadulterated philosophical questions Mamardashvili was addressing in this work, it is obvious that he was also struggling to make his "sketch" acceptable—or at least, hopefully, sufficiently incomprehensible—to his scientific superiors. In this he failed and was once again fired.

And yet, although in conversation Mamardashvili did attribute the difficulty of his writing to his efforts to sidestep censorship,[20] it is worth asking to what extent this is true. Epelboin, to whom he admitted the strategic nature of his obscure style, also notes that, reading him, she found it "very difficult and even impossible to understand the thoughts of the author (*if there were any* [my italics]), to grasp them behind their Aesopic language," although, she goes on to say, in conversation Mamardashvili was "direct, laconic, and precise."[21] Mamardashvili's written opus, furthermore, turned out to be "very difficult and even impossible to understand" not only for the authorities and for young nonphilosophy students like Epelboin but also for many of his immediate colleagues and friends, both in his own time and later.[22] The query, hence, is whether the obscurity was all about the Aesopic language and whether there could at all be an easy way to approach the problems Mamardashvili was trying to resolve in the 1970s.

The fact is that, in sharp contrast to the impenetrability of his writing, the series of lectures on ancient and modern philosophy, on introduction to philosophy, on Descartes, Kant, Proust, and so on, that Mamardashvili delivered to various audiences (not necessarily students of philosophy) at different universities in the late 1970s and in the 1980s, are not only straightforward, lucid, and enticing but also sometimes bluntly defiant of the regime in its theoretical, political, and everyday dimensions. The lectures were tape-recorded and not published until much later, but, although their daring could be the obvious reason for Mamardashvili's forced academic nomadism, they nevertheless illustrate how much freer oral performance could be in those years. The Socratic stance in these lectures is legible in the published versions that we can read today: Mamardashvili is employing his formidable rhetorical skills to engage his audience in the pursuit of philosophical questions—to which he believes human beings are naturally predisposed—while at the same time implying that the pursuit of such questions is the one viable approach to the proper settling of issues of the polis, of the "agora," as he puts it, of the political.

So was this "philosopher of the spoken word" the "true" Mamardashvili as Epelboin, but also a keen thinker like Mikhail Ryklin, seem to have believed? If so, was he offering the "belated flowers" of metaphysics?[23] Or does the shift from the "obscurity" of his writing to his "direct, laconic, and precise" talking raise, perhaps, other questions? If the obscurity was a strategy to sidestep ideological censorship, could the accessibility of oral presentation be also a strategy to overcome this other censorship, the one of common sense, of the doxa? If so, did the coming to the fore of pragmatic pedagogical and political concerns in his oral output displace, trivialize, or perhaps even erase the innovative ideas proposed in Mamardashvili's writing? While the thorough, more scrupulous answer to these questions will have to wait, at this point I will be guided by the following presuppositions. First, in spite of the "heterogeneous philosophemes" that make up his work and despite his own mournful hints about this work as a sort of philosophical "miscarriage," there is continuity between the written and the oral output of Mamardashvili.[24]

Second, there may be a purely contingent biographical factor at play in Mamardashvili's shift from (predominantly) written to (predominantly) oral genres—powerful friends who supported him died; he lost one job after another; and so on. And yet, the fact is that Mamardashvili's shift toward the oral coincides with the logic that shaped the political climate of the last decade of communism, which I have already discussed. It is, therefore, impossible not to see Mamardashvili's turn to orality as driven by—and giving its force to—the time's winds of change. Seen in the reverse order, this is the logic that explains why in the 1980s and the 1990s Mamardashvili was perceived as an "oral philosopher," while now a reassessment is deemed necessary that would highlight his written opus.

THE FABRIC OF COMMUNICATION

In fact—and this is hardly surprising—there is a lot that Mamardashvili does say about the written and the oral. Thus, his presentation on the "European responsibility" begins by apologizing about the inevitable mistakes he will make speaking in French,[25] and yet, speak he must, he goes on to say, because he is "unable to read a text that has already been written."[26] This claim might be—and has been—interpreted as a personal trait of the philosopher as a man "not of the written word." And yet, given the complicated and ultimately dubious standing of Mamardashvili as an oral philosopher tout court, it seems worthwhile pointing out that he did not say he was unable to write a text. He said he was unable to read one that had already been written. In his lectures, Mamardashvili offers various examples, from Descartes to Wittgenstein, of thinkers who did not find writing imperative and who would frequently prefer conversations, letters, or notes, to fully developed texts. Nonetheless, he observes that we are lucky that Kant did write down his "experience with being."[27] What matters, in writing or talking, is the "movement of thought."[28] Reading to an audience a text that has already been written makes no sense because it would arrest this movement. For the unfolding of thought one does not need to stand in awe of finished texts—one might write huge volumes like Kant or Proust but one might very well jot notes, write letters, give lectures, and talk with friends. This explication applies also to Mamardashvili's discussions of Plato as the emblem of the most extreme distrust of writing. The point is Plato's conviction that thought *can only be remembered* in writing. Plato distrusted writing because he did not see it as the medium for the movement of thought.

In a further concurrence with the seminar trends, Mamardashvili states in *The Arrow of Knowledge* that we should return to the original understanding of dialectics as dialogue and communication, while in the lectures on *The Aesthetics of Thought* he endorses Plato's views on the maieutic powers of dialogue. The peculiar twist here is that Mamardashvili is not a believer in communication, at least not in the sense of conveying what one thinks or knows to somebody else. He repeatedly interrupts his lectures to note that there is no telling as to what exactly his audience will haul out of his words. They might completely miss his meaning and he would never know. In fact, "the problem of communication as the problem of the 'other' is a spurious problem," he claims in *The Arrow of Knowledge*.[29] Thought is as much a secret for its author as for its receiver. "Anything we can say about the world hangs in the fabric spread out between subjects."[30] This fabric weaves us together in a divine setting, which—and here we come close to the "unnaturalness" intrinsic to man—loosens the connections pertaining to the natural order. All we can hope for is that we relate, together with the other, to this "comprehension topos."

So why communication? It is precisely because knowledge cannot be transmitted. Understanding is a *state*, a tension like the tension produced by the two opposite sides of the bow: It is something that emerges in the middle of the bowstring whose ends will never meet.

> Let us take the most ancient dialectical image, the image of Heraclites' bow. It is my favorite. Why does the arrow fly? It flies because the tensions of the two ends of the bow pull in opposite directions. For Heraclites, the bow is also a symbol of harmony—harnessing something in one, although what we have in fact is forces acting in different directions. And yet, precisely their opposite pull is the condition for something positive, for a real event, a breakthrough.[31]
>
> In the sphere of material instruments such a perfect artifact is the bow whose function is to produce a specific action, one that is com-

> plete and full in itself (and is not produced by nature). Now, our interest lies with the artifacts producing thought . . . like an arrow that has been set off by the man and is flying toward its target. *It* is flying; I do not move it with my step by step thinking.[32]

The image of the bow is important for Mamardashvili because, along with its remarkable dialectical features, it is an instrument, something artificial, an artifact. We cannot will an act of thought; we cannot will an event; we cannot will change; and neither can we will ourselves as human: What we can do is construct instruments producing states that might set off the arrow to fly. We have to engender *not* the thought (we cannot do this) but its source; we need to engender the engendering, create the creating. The "created creating" is a "state." A state is one of the terms describing the work of "noogenic machines" (artifacts), which subtend events.[33]

The task, then, is to craft "noogenic machines," devices and gadgets, which might trigger a free act and in which, therefore, the possibility of an event is folded. Communication is such a machine, a Heraclites' bow. Tension, effort, flight, breakthrough, nondeductibility and unpredictability, irreversible change, the new: The work of communication is not to produce understanding but the state (the pulling of the ends of the bow) that might engender an act of thought and, with it, man. This is Mamardashvili's reading of Marx's early idea that the essence of man is communication. It means that "the human is principally plural, that the human is a communicating plurality. This is why the essence of man is not a fact existing by itself; it exists only insofar as the human person maintains, reproduces, and preserves communication. If the support and the reproduction of communication do not exist, there is no man. There is simply an animal."[34]

And so, while Mamardashvili does not seem to set a principal difference between writing and talking in their capacity to sustain the movement of thought or to (not) induce understanding, live conversation seems to offer a better illustration of the "fabric of communication," the "comprehension topos" that thought as an act leaves behind like the arrow set off by the bowstring. Mamardashvili's turn to orality might hence be regarded as a performative explication—and, in view of desired impending changes, a hope for intensification—of this crucial setting. This is where the effort, the work, and, with them, the responsibility come into play.

Glancing back for the last time at the Dubrovnik drama discussed in the second chapter, we can now add another perspective to the misery that the failure of communication there produced. In the light of Mamardashvili's thought, what fails with the failure of communication is not comprehension; so much is clear. What fails is the tension that produces thought as an act—that produces change as an event—that produces man. In the parabolic Dubrovnik happening, he may have been finally convinced that man is finished, after all.

DESIRE: MAN AS TRAGEDY

There is an aspect of the anthropological machine, as discussed by Agamben, that becomes apparent in its absence: desire. The "desoeuvrement" of desire forms the arch above the flaccid proximity of the shepherd and the nymph, with whom, in *The Open*, we bid farewell to human nature. Retroactively, this "desoeuvrement" brings into focus the role that desire plays in the operation of the anthropological machine. Pico della Mirandola, the Renaissance thinker whom Agamben quotes apropos the undefined nature of man, makes it clear that, between the animals and the angels, it is the passionate desire for the life of the angels, which is the proper choice for man, the creature without identity. Wanting to be more than what man is, makes man what he is. Man, as a recent study of the emergence of tragedy in the context of Athenian democracy succinctly puts it, is the animal that *wants* to be human. Performed as sacrificial ritual before acquiring a new level thanks to the dissemination of writing with the ensuing rise of the political and the tragic, the differentiation of the "politicon" from the "zoon" remains nevertheless as problematic as it is painful. The tragic "effect of the real" testifies to the fact that man knows himself to be animal but wants himself to be human. The dynamic of this wanting subtends the tragedy.[35]

If being human amounts to desiring to be human (which, therefore, man is not), being human turns out to be suspended in the mode of an inaccessible object. Herewith lies the paradox in Pico della Mirandola's statement: To be human one must passionately try to be more than human (an angel, a drinking companion to the gods). The sublimating logic of passion as the coincidence of desire and suffering rips open the discrepancy between the demand and its impossible satisfaction; it inhabits the incongruity between being human as a transcendent objective and the animal that we are. This, in its turn, means that being human never quite happens. Or, rather, it happens as either too little, or too much, too soon, or too late: Insofar as "tragedy is essentially the pain of [the] difference"[36] between the demand and its impossible satisfaction, it happens as tragedy, and it happens in the *hero*. This is to say it happens most often in death and as death.

"There are many wondrous things, and yet nothing is more wondrous than man," states the chorus at the beginning of the paradigmatic tragedy *Antigone*. The one thing, the chorus goes on to say, which still reduces man to the status of the animal, is death, By the end of the play, however, the heroine Antigone will prove the wondrousness of man precisely by dying, by turning death into a place where mere biological life is separated from the human capacity to surpass it. In death, in the very place of death (the tomb where she is buried alive), she incorporates the sublime Thing that distinguishes the human from the animal.[37] Tragedy is the violence done to the animal by the incorporation of the human: The effect of humanity (as the desired Thing) on the animal (that man knows himself to be) is an excruciating and yet uplifting suffering.[38] The inoperativeness of the anthropological machine, of the machine, which separates man from animal, would hence imply a suspension of the tragic incorporation and, with it, a decline of the tragic mode per se. The human no longer takes place in the desire to be human. We end up with, as Agamben has it, a humanization of the animal and an animalization of man. The question is, does this mean that this impossible object, the human, no longer happens at all? Or could the brotherhood with the animal be indicative of other trouble?

A NOTE ON THE SECOND SEX

In Agamben's book, the female side to things appears first in the figure of the egg-laying tick and the second time in the figure of the nymph, thus not quite on the side of the human. It would seem that Simone de Beauvoir's project for the becoming of woman was caught up in the process that put an end to the "human exception." Could there be a necessary connection between the two? After all, as Beauvoir herself analyzed in *The Second Sex*, the metaphysical operation that differentiated man from nature was largely coincidental with the one that differentiated man from woman. If woman would be equal to man, what's the point of man trying to be different from the animal? This conjunction manifested itself with the very appearance of Mary Wollstonecraft's *A Vindication of the Rights of Woman* in 1792: It was swiftly followed by a satire called A *Vindication of the Rights of Brutes*. The satire was written by the former landlord to the Wollstonecraft family, Thomas Taylor, a translator of Plato and Aristotle and a Neoplatonist, who clearly thought all this a big joke. Today, it is not clear on whom the joke has been played. In any case, at the time of the emergence of feminism and, joke or no joke, of animal rights, in literature, yet another thing happened. The automaton and the artificial creature made their entrance with a flare that would become the very definition of the uncanny in a century or so. As if to make this genealogical juncture more conspicuous, the creator of *Frankenstein* was the daughter of the author of *The Vindication of the Rights of Woman*.

AN UNFINISHED PROJECT

"The Cylons were created by man. They rebelled. They evolved. They look and feel human. Some of them are programmed to think they are human. There are many copies. And they have a plan."[39]

This is the intro to the first season (beginning with the second episode) of *Battlestar Galactica,* a formidable recent remake of a 1970s TV series about rebellious machines, which destroy the humanity that has created them and hunt the remaining survivors all over the universe. On a grand scale and in epic proportions the movie offers yet another version of the plot of the artificial creature, which turns into a nemesis of its creator, a plot that has been with us ever since Frankenstein's Monster opened his watery eyes on a dreary night in December almost two hundred years ago. Unlike the ugly Monster, however, or E. T. A. Hoffmann's doll-like Olympia, unlike earlier literary generations of robots with creaking joints and flat metallic voices, the "evolved" Cylons are practically indistinguishable from humans: They bleed; they sweat; they make love; they believe in God: In fact, some of them believe they are God's messengers to their sinful creators. There are differences, to be sure: One of them is that there are many copies of each Cylon "model"; another one is that each copy can "resurrect" by "downloading" into a new body, which makes the Cylons all but immortal. Also, they cannot reproduce "naturally," so achieving a human-Cylon hybrid—a prophesied messianic "face of the things to come"—is one of the objectives that drive their perverse scheming.

And yet, human, all too human they are, whether programmed to think they are human or not, and furthermore, some of them *want* to be human, going to such lengths as being ready to give up immortality. . . . If you look and feel human, and if you are programmed to think you are human, how would anyone know the difference? The film tracks the dwindling emotional, intellectual, and political distinctions and finally takes the bunch of surviving humans and Cylons, including the hybrid baby, Hera, to a prehistoric Earth where they are clearly to become the future mankind's half-human half-machine gods.

The question is whether the standstill of the anthropological machine producing man through his differentiation from the animal might be owing not really to inoperativeness but to a major shift in the place and mode of its operation. "Are you alive?"—are the first words pronounced in *Battlestar Galactica*. Being alive—sharing the mysterious drop of blood with the tick—in short, the animalization of man—could be a last resort of the creature without proper identity, which fears it might be . . . a machine. Differentiating man from the machine, rather than the animal, cannot but affect the status of the animal. In *Do Androids Dream of Electric Sheep* Philip K. Dick offers a striking insight into this novel framework: In a civilization of vegetarians, where killing an animal (there are too few left, to be sure) is unthinkable and possessing one is the most coveted sign of success in life, artificial quasi human beings are the hard laborers, the enemy, the prey, the sacrificial victim. *"Who gets sacrificed?"*[40]

This turn of events might be a bit ironic insofar as Descartes, famously and perhaps wrongfully, reinterpreted Aristotle's notion of the automaton in a manner that caused animals (but also man in La Metrie's *Man a Machine*) to be viewed as "mere" mechanisms and machines. Animals were supposed to be the automata, the mechanisms whose functioning did not need a soul or some mysterious life force to be explained. The great objective of the French engineering genius Vaucanson,[41] who captured the imagination of his epoch, was to construct a "physiological automaton"—an objective, certainly motivated by the desire to take an empirical stand in the debate. (In this, he predictably did not succeed, and one of his remarkable toys—a duck that could eat and defecate, supposedly digesting the food—was a sham.) The autonomization of the automaton, however, its subtraction from man and animal in the imaginary but also in scientific pursuits, had the effect of confronting man from the other side, so to say, from a side excluding whatever man and animal had in common.

The artificial creature, consequently, does not come to represent the mechanical essence of the animal, but, on the contrary, it emerges as the offspring of an ambition to construct the zero point of subjectivity at the juncture where "the spiritual would directly spring from the material"[42] and thus forgo life and animality altogether. From the very inception, Mary Shelley offered two powerful metaphors for this bracketing of "life": Frankenstein's Monster is put together from parts of corpses, and he is motherless—he has a father only.

As the fruit of an immediate conjunction of spirit and automaton, the creature is structured around a twofold surprise. In the first type of surprise, what looks human turns out to be a machine. This revelation may take place as a more or less brutal mutilation so that the creature—to quote C-3PO from *Star Wars*—"shows its parts."[43] Such is the paradigmatic scene in Hoffmann's *The Sandman* where Nathanael, who, not knowing that the Olympia doll is an automaton, falls in love but then witnesses her dismantling by her makers. In "The Mask" Stanislaw Lem remakes this uncanny scene, more or less tongue in cheek, with his protagonist cutting her human body in front of a mirror and revealing the mechanical insides exactly at the moment when her destined lover and victim enters the room with a bunch of flowers.

The second type of surprise comes when what is known to be mechanical turns out to be human. This may take place in a number of ways: For example, the machine falls in love, which, for the object of this love, is not necessarily a matter for rejoicing. Or, even more typically, whether enamored or not, the machine rebels against its creator. The creature, that is, confronts its creator with a surprise, as the cliché has it, gets out of control by doing, feeling, thinking, and so on—things that were not planned by the creator; To put it in the words of *Battlestar Galactica*'s intro, *it* "has a plan." It is noteworthy, however, that the surprise tends to precede anything the creature says or does: Thus Frankenstein, although never wavering in his macabre step-by-step creation of the Monster, is terribly surprised the moment the Monster is "switched on" by lightning and, from this moment on, keeps being surprised until the end. My most recent example, *Battlestar Galactica,* also begins with a surprise—in fact, a number of them: after a forty-year truce between humans and Cylons, the human ambassador is expecting that once again the Cylons will send no representative to the yearly meeting envisioned by the treaty. However, the door opens, and two clumsy metallic robots make way for a tall blond young woman who walks magnificently toward the human ambassador to ask him whether he is alive and signal with a kiss the beginning of human destruction. In this case, the nature of the surprise is thrown into relief by the juxtaposition of the robots the humans created and the supermodel girl into which they have "evolved": There is an excessiveness, a too muchness of the human in the artificial being, which was neither called for, nor foreseen.

Although this "too muchness" frequently (but not necessarily) signals a threat to the creators, structurally it resembles the comic *en plus*: As with comedy, we receive an unexpected surplus, a surplus that we did not ask for. As Alenka Zupančič points out in *The Odd One In*, with comedy—but this is precisely what happens with the plots of man-made creatures—not only do we not get what we asked for; on top of that (and not instead) we get something we haven't even asked for.[44] The robot can be seen precisely as the comic *en plus* that provides an unforeseen surplus humanity to the "animal that wants to be human."

The artificial creature, furthermore, resembles comedy in two other crucial respects. First, it is based on montage: Like the comic object, the artificial creature is put together of various fake materials that sooner or later have to show; the gadgets have to pop up. A comic example proper is the constant disassembling and reassembling of C-3PO in *Star Wars.* Even in *Battlestar Galactica* where the machines "evolve" to "look and feel human" and where the central problem is precisely the ungraspable phantom of the vanishing difference between the humans and the machines, there comes a moment when one of the Cylon protagonists wires her veins into a computer network exposing her "parts."

The second prominent resemblance is reduplication: If the comic works through reduplication, so does the artificial creature, which functions as the double of man. The more indistinguishable from the human being, the more clearly the imitation raises the question of man's identity and the more man has to struggle for his difference from this disquieting impostor. Thus, the human emerges not through the painful separation of man from animal but through the *entre-deux*, the in-between of man and his own artificial semblance.

The point is not to claim that artificial creatures belong to comedy as a genre, which is quite obviously not the case. True, the comic reversal is never far, as parodic versions of *Frankenstein* demonstrate. Notably, *Battlestar Galactica* avoided a number of disastrous possibilities in its brushes with the sublime thanks to the saving graces of humor and by switching to a frankly comic finale. Frequently acting as a threat to humanity, robots deploy the paradox of the doppelgänger, who can appear either as the comic twin or as the annihilating double, thus stalking the edge between comedy proper and the uncanny.[45] The point in this case, however, is to single out the mechanism of reduplication that acts through montage and that posits an altogether different "anthropological machine." Instead of separating man from animal, this machine proliferates man's fake doubles. Since repetition, stubborn return, unlimited "downloadability" characterizes it, there is plenty of evidence that this machine does not work through desire but on the level of the drive. This would explain Mamardashvili's claim that "man is impossible, but he happens": At the level of the zero-man, of the absent subject, like the arrow set off from the bow, man happens thanks to us but without us.

If so, the positions, which were represented here via Agamben and Mamardashvili, would be both true and false. Yes, the anthropological machine has come to a standstill, and man is no longer busy separating himself from the animal; the tragic mechanism that struck the animal with the sublime lightning of incorporated humanity is inoperative. And yes, man keeps being an unfinished creature, engaged with his noogenic gadgets, driven by his own creations, the created creating, that tend to look more and more like him—or he, like them. And what about the fabric of communication? Is it, perhaps, literally there, as the Web? In any case, at this vanishing point of the gone communist heterotopia, heterotopian homonymy turns out to be more homonymous than heterotopian. While this is not necessarily a laughing matter, we can nevertheless propose the hypothesis that man as an unfinished project has taken a comic—or, indeed, uncanny—turn.

Addendum: The Discretions of Inverted Theory

Unfortunately, and contrary to what is currently assumed about the proverbial ivory-tower independence of thinkers, no other human capacity is so vulnerable [as thinking], and it is in fact far easier to act under conditions of tyranny than it is to think.

—Hannah Arendt, *The Human Condition*

In one of his discussions of the uncanny, Mladen Dolar notes that "in order for the mirror image to contain the object *a*, a wink or a nod is enough."[1] Imagine, he suggests, that you look at your image in the mirror and the image closes its eyes. In what follows—a supplement rather than a conclusion—the startling occurrence of such a wink in Julia Kristeva's novel *Murder in Byzantium* will add the problem of accruing contexts to the problem of fading or elusive contexts that has subtended my ruminations so far. This ostensibly contrasting problem (rather than modes of cunning intellectual resistance, it will summon up modes of compliance and spiritual surrender; rather than the glittering mirror of intellectual utopia, it will uphold the dark glass of the regime's cloaked reality, the dreaded secret services) will nevertheless pose the same question: How can this vulnerable human capacity, the capacity *to think*—so much more vulnerable, according to Arendt, than the capacity to act—be sustained in adverse circumstances? As it is bound to do, the Real in this story pops up seemingly out of nowhere—in the unlikely propinquity of a Byzantine princess from the eleventh and twelfth centuries.

FADING AND ACCRUING

And so, there is, on the one hand, the obvious issue of the lost context. The vanishing context washes away parabolic levels of meaning that were evident in their own epoch but that would be available today only after careful and uncertain unraveling. It would be far too easy if the obscurities were somehow marked. In most cases, however, the parabolic meaning, the double bottom of the message, is so seamlessly blended with its surface that, in its own time, censorship would not be able to pinpoint it without taking the risk of exposing its own "dirty" thoughts, and, today, an unprejudiced reader would never suspect a trick or a trap. Tzotcho Boiadjiev's statement quoted in the introduction—

> Plato's ideal is not mystical silence but the complete unfurling of the element of speech. . . . The most profound knowledge is not achieved through solitary mystical illumination but through an intense cognitive effort, which is always carried out with the other.[2]

—would slickly be read today as a commentary on Plato, which, of course, it is. In its own epoch, however, this statement had additional implications.

1. The knowledge offered in the collective modes of the official discourse (the endless speeches that filled public space) was not worth even mentioning. There was no need to deny it: Ignoring it was sufficiently eloquent. Quietly disregarding the clichés of dogma used to be loaded with meaning that will be totally lost today.
2. Solitary mystical illumination was a possible corrective to the regime's valorization of noisy heroic collectivity. It could take the form of what used to be called internal emigration, or it could find recourse to the New Age niches

that the Bulgarian dictator's daughter had succeeded in half-legitimizing before her own mysterious demise. Rejecting the corrective of silence as inadequate is part of Boiadjiev's hidden agenda.

3. And finally, there is the idea that has preoccupied me throughout this book: the cognitive effort always carried out with the other through the "complete unfurling of the element of speech." Apart from being a commentary on Plato, the notion of complete unfurling is a reflection of prevalent practices at the time the book was written. The word I translate here as "profound" has the slightly obsolete meaning of "hidden" and is habitually used to translate *deus absconditus*, the "hidden god." It thus introduces the idea of concealment and secrecy as the very secret key to the multiple layers of the text where it appears. In its contemporary usage, however, the word most often means "intimate," that is, something calling for discretion. Not collective hullabaloo and not solitary silence but discreet togetherness in a profound knowledge: Plato's "unwritten doctrine" (which is the book's title) is transformed into a cryptogram of his commentator's credo. As pointed out before, the author Tzotcho Boiadjiev defined this procedure, shared by his audience, as "drawing the dialogical projections of one's time in an unusual direction:"[3] a procedure which, as much as I could, I have tried to follow in this book.

However, along with the vanishing context of the "transparent book"[4] of the epoch's cryptography there is the problem of an accruing context. The accrual takes place through the dramatic collapses and shifts in perspective that result from the making public of the communist secret services archives: a tortuous and protracted (in Bulgaria, at least) process that, two decades after the fall of communism, has not been completed yet. Whether properly preserved or not, whether properly read or not, the amorphous shadows of those texts written by intellectuals to denounce other intellectuals and addressed solely to the discreet ear of the secret services cannot but provoke another type of stratification, symmetrical and opposed to the one described above. While the first case implies a togetherness that allows multiple "transparent" layers of meaning in a single text, denunciations have to be as straightforward as can be and are intended for a single hidden addressee. Of course, it has often been claimed, and in many cases this has been probably true, that denunciations could be no less duplicitous, cunning, attempting to play a double game, and, in fact, not do what they purportedly did (i.e., betray friends and colleagues). And yet, whatever the subjective investments, clearly we are dealing here with two divergent regimes of "discretion." In the first instance, the transparent concealment of the multilayered parabolic language is driven by a totally indiscreet impulse: the impulse to become public and, in fact, to join an overarching and absolute public domain. In the second case, a shamelessly direct and indiscreet message was subtended by the hope it would never reach an ear other than the ear of the secret services; that is, it relied on unconditional discretion. No wonder that, in the initial turmoil when the changes began, one of the first brazen events was the setting on fire of the central state archives. Who did it and what precisely perished or, perhaps, did not perish in the flames is a matter of discretion to this very day.

FROM THE DOME OF BEING TO CRIME FICTION

By migrating to France in 1965 Julia Kristeva left behind these ruses of discretion. In the course of twenty-five years or so—in fact, until the collapse of the Eastern bloc system—Bulgaria is hardly ever mentioned in her writing. One notable exception is the painful—and rather unusual for her—confessional tone of "The Novel as Polylogue," in which she states that she speaks "in French and about literature because of Yalta."[5] By "Yalta" she means the division of Europe after World War II, which was negotiated by the "Big Three" (Churchill, Roosevelt, and

Stalin) at the Yalta conference in 1945 and which determined Bulgaria's fate as part of the communist Eastern bloc.

Kristeva has sometimes been reprimanded for her reticence on her Bulgarian past: According to Gayatri Chakravorty Spivak, Kristeva's "own pre-history in Bulgaria is not even a shadow under the harsh light of the Parisian voice."[6] And yet, it would be more accurate to say that the Bulgarian shadow has passed into its own regime of discretion: into two modes of discretion, to be more precise. On the one hand, this is the mode of an implicit *narrative* in Kristeva's theoretical works from the 1970s and 1980s. As I have demonstrated elsewhere, her theoretical preoccupations in these works surreptitiously unfold a hushed story: the story of an irrecoverable lost territory, of an immortal sorrow, of a disconsolate wandering. The ciphers that mark the trajectory of this irredeemable sadness envelop the map of the lost motherland, which, although unnamed and invisible, emits powerful idealizing energies.[7]

No less palpable is a purely theoretical shadow of the lost territory. Kristeva's early writing—from *Semeiotiké* (1969) to *Polylogue* (1977)—is characterized by a broad interdisciplinarity, a taste for the exact sciences, a penchant for neologisms, and—in keeping with the claim that philosophy is the art of fabricating concepts, as Deleuze and Guattari would later put it—a profusion of newly formed or refunctionalized terms, many of which acquired wide circulation. Her tough terminological machinery addressing a plethora of literary and cultural issues through a multiplicity of schools and disciplines, while typical of the French but also of the international intellectual scene at the time, is nevertheless marked by an excessiveness whose precise lineage remains nameless. It includes, of course, the Russian formalists (criticized yet thoroughly read) and Bakhtin, whose integration into the French theoretical discussions owes a lot to the rightful, or maybe wrongful, as sometimes has been claimed, mediation of Kristeva. Even more pertinent in this respect would be the figure of the legendary Tartu semiotician Yuri Lotman who edited, since 1964, a journal bearing the same title spelled in Greek as Kristeva's early book—Σημειωτική (*Semeiotiké*). However, it is little known in Bulgaria—and not at all elsewhere, I believe — that Kristeva's very first book appeared in 1964 in Bulgaria before she left for France. Its title is *Characteristic Trends in Twentieth-Century Western Literature*. In this book the twenty-three-year-old author discusses the "characteristic trends" in a manner characteristic of the time and place: On the surface, this is a critique of decadent Western literature and philosophy; in effect, this is a smart and seductive presentation of authors and books otherwise unavailable because of censorship. The book is slim and encyclopedically concise and yet striking in terms of both erudition and analytic incisiveness. It shares a lot of common ground with a number of contemporaneous Bulgarian authors, including earlier and later works by Tzvetan Stoyanov, the author of "On Good Conversations," to whom I have referred a number of times. In Kristeva's first novel, *The Samurai*, Stoyanov enters the stage as the protagonist's former boyfriend Dan. Although Bulgaria is as yet not named in the novel, Dan's appearance in it can be regarded as a sort of relay point: marking Kristeva's connection to the obscure Bulgarian intellectual scene and the henceforth growing visibility of Bulgaria in Kristeva's writing.

Dan, as described by Kristeva in *The Samurai*, "knew practically every language and had read all the important works ever written in English, German, French, Russian, Spanish, and Italian, from the dim distant past up to the present. He was a glutton for culture and had absorbed all the great writers, philosophers, and poets. Like some representative of the Age of Enlightenment strayed into an obscure country and another age, he bestowed his erudition on the ignoramuses around him in the form of skeptical parables. To him Olga [Kristeva's alter ego in *The Samurai*] owed all she knew about Shakespeare and Cervantes, Browning and Emily Dickinson, Mallarmé and Faulkner."[8]

The meeting does not go so well for Dan, who is hoping to convince Olga to return to her native country. Dan's feeling is that Olga has moved to the "other side"— which would be true, if we speak of Tzvetan Stoyanov, not only in terms of Kristeva's defecting to France (and, as Dan points out, to an easy game of political protest as opposed to its deadly earnestness at home) but also in terms of theoretical debates around structuralism back in Bulgaria. What concerns me at this point, however, is, beyond such specifics, the phrase "glutton for culture [who] had absorbed all the great writers, philosophers, and poets." It could very well be applied to the voracity of Kristeva's own early project, already visible in her youthful Bulgarian book and most thoroughly exemplified in *Semeiotiké* (still considered by many Bulgarian scholars to be her best book) and the *The Revolution in Poetic Language* (both books are as yet not translated in their totality in English, precisely, I guess, because of their too-muchness). This voracity seems to share a common platform not only with Dan/Tzvetan Stoyanov but with various and sometimes conflicting trends in Bulgarian theoretical thinking at the time. As I pointed out in the Introduction, the impossibility for Bulgarian thinkers to participate in the "horizontal" international debates sought resolution in an attempt to assume a meta-position and integrate vertically the summa of theoretical thought.[9] The Bulgarian theoretical field was hence characterized, even before the decade of the seminar, by "dome-ness"—where the homonym of dome, *dom*, means "home," implying something like "Theory is the dome of being." The proper translation of dome in Bulgarian as *svod*, however, might refer to the architectural structure, to the sky as firmament, to a library catalogue of catalogues, and, last but, perhaps, not least, to *svat* and *svodnik*, matchmaker and go-between, which would pinpoint the propensity of dome-ness to bring together likely and unlikely theoretical bedfellows. The mediation and the effort to assemble discourses is not a matter of simple addition, however, as one of Kristeva's Bulgarian peers Radosvet Kolarov has recently claimed through the concept of transmodality.[10] The transmodal idea is an idea that passes from one discourse into another, from one discipline into another, and from one epoch into another. In the course of these transitions it acquires specific auras, which may coalesce or diffract and altogether make it unrecognizable: Its various reincarnations can even deny each other or, indeed, completely ignore each other. Going beyond these auras to unveil the sameness, however, which a ravenous theoretician is bound to do, would have the paradoxical effect of disclosing dynamics, process, metamorphosis, and singular points of torsion and inflexion. Kristeva's early work—but also Tzvetan Todorov's, viewed in this perspective—stands as the visible (French) articulation of this agenda.

In the context of communist repression the agenda was, ultimately, a defiant faith in the material power of thought. In Kristeva's work, the transmodal invariant of this faith takes the form of a program for finding a new universality in the perspective of the singular and the unique: from the "revolution in poetic language" to the "intimate revolution" in her recent writing. But, we might note at this point, with a *différance.* Kristeva herself attributes this difference to her encounter with Freud, whom she did not have in her communist suitcase. (Freud is, in fact, discussed in her Bulgarian book, so she probably means Freud's absence in terms of psychoanalytic practice.) Consequently, Kristeva's focus on the reverse of signifying practices, on the semiotic traversing of symbolic structures, on the subject-in-process, and on the site of the production of subjectivity and signification evolves as an answer to a number of poststructuralist aporias concerning universality, identity, and linguisticality. In her early work Kristeva terms her method for exploring this underside of signification semanalysis, which amounts to describing "the signifying phenomenon, or signifying phenomena, while analyzing, criticizing, and dissolving 'phenomenon,' 'meaning,' and 'signifier.' "[11]

This corrosive—as Kristeva herself defines it—procedure obviously runs counter to the procedure that fabricates new concepts: It dissolves them. If philosophy is the fabrication of concepts, what would be the discipline of dissolving them? Wouldn't Kristeva's theoretical project be overrun by an antitheoretical drive? Less dramatically put, the very logic of semanalysis as the decomposition of meaning and signifier calls for a metamorphosis into the narrative and the fictional, and, ultimately, into the (intimate) revolutions of poetry. The fictional dimension of Kristeva's theoretical works, which she repeatedly highlights,[12] is therefore a spontaneous and inevitable product of the semanalytic dissolution of conceptuality and a logical result of her method.

If Kristeva's fictionality materializes in a reversal of the philosophical procedure that invents concepts, her novels—which she began writing comparatively late in her career—cannot be made of the material that novels are usually made of. Nor are they similar to the philosophical novel as variously exemplified by authors such as Voltaire or Thomas Mann in whose works philosophical ideas are embodied and provided with a story. Some studies have claimed that Kristeva's novels are allegorical in the sense of Benjamin's analysis of the German *Trauerspiel,*[13] yet it should be stressed that Benjamin discusses allegory as the life of irresistible decay and as the form that finds its perfection in ruin.[14] If we can describe Kristeva's novels as allegorical, it is because, in them, allegory emerges effectively in the decay of concepts (as the growing nails of a corpse, to use Benjamin's metaphor). As the site of conceptual dissolution, the body that ideas in Kristeva's novels gravitate toward tends to be a dead body; and the story they are granted tends toward carnage. Ergo, murder is their subject matter and their genre, crime fiction, whose nature is even stranger than it looks.

B&B

Inversion as the site of alteration of theory into fiction might be conceived in Lacan's terms, as a specular reversal and as a transformation in the imaginary. The imaginary acts as a barrier and causes discourse to be transmitted in an inverted form.[15] One could also refer to Merab Mamardashvili's elaboration of Marx's idea of the *verwandelte Form*, especially with Mamardashvili's emphasis on the erasure of causal links and structural connections in objects that have been effectively cut off—and hence function as a concealment of—the operations that produced them.[16] In Kristeva's case, where a message transmitted as theory returns as fiction, the inversion involves a turning around of the said and the unsaid, a change of guard, so to speak (with reference to Derrida's gloss of Hegel's *Aufhebung*) of mystery and discretion.

This amounts to saying that crime and mystery in Kristeva's novels articulate the unsaid of her theory. What comes to the surface is propelled by the specific type of discretion that characterizes Kristeva's theoretical thinking. As already pointed out, this discretion revolves around a muffled narrative of exile, of wandering and seeking for a lost object and a nameless territory. At one pertinent point Kristeva relates this silent story to the "mute sister of philosophy."[17] A murderous secret, a dark sorrow, a shadowy country, a restless search, and an asymbolic feminine subject: In the novels after *The Samurai* the hidden parable becomes explicit, and the narrative finds its fictional buttress in Kristeva's protagonist Stephanie Delacour, a perennial foreigner and "a globe-trotting investigative reporter-detective."[18]

Stephanie Delacour weaves together the multifaceted reversals that take place in Kristeva's fiction and in her theoretical writing contemporaneous with the novels. Up until the beginning of the nineties Kristeva is frequently criticized for focusing her research on male artists. It is claimed that her study of the semiotic and the maternal privileges male (homosexual, or not) creativity. This is in many ways true: The book on Proust can be seen as a massive summing up of this trend. Critics, however, overlook the fact that Kristeva's theoretical figuration includes herself as relentless explorer of the matricidal alchemy of male artistic subjectivities. Fiction allows this discreet fact to become visible: And so, the theoretician jumps on stage as detective-reporter Stephanie Delacour. In the second half of the 1990s Kristeva adds a further and important twist to this change: The trilogy on "female genius" dedicated to three women excelling in different fields (Hannah Arendt, Melanie Klein, and

Colette) focuses on female creativity, thus reversing the cultural ramifications of the matricidal phantasmatics. The appearance of Anna Comnena, a Byzantine princess of the eleventh and twelfth centuries—the first woman historiographer and, according to Kristeva's novel, the first woman intellectual in European history, author of the fifteen volumes of the *Alexiad*, dealing with the historical events of her own tempestuous times—as a pivotal figure in *Murder in Byzantium* is indicative of this shift toward a female object of scientific interest, veneration, and transtemporal love. Kristeva's most recent book on Saint Teresa indicates that this interest continues to evolve.

Similar processes occur with respect to the "lost territory" of Kristeva's earlier oeuvre. Almost never mentioned before *The Samurai,* Kristeva's country of origin, Bulgaria, becomes more and more explicitly present in her subsequent writing. This growing presence of the lost object, however, takes the form of a veritable return of the abject: Bulgaria is depicted as a typical waste product of the age of "Santa Vărvara," Kristeva's fictional representation of the negative effects of globalization, of the society of the spectacle, the domination of images, corruption, fundamentalism, and terrorism, and, ultimately, of the decline of thinking. The controversial essay "Bulgaria, My Suffering," written in 1995, is emblematic: From the poverty of language ("this poor language of sensitive peasants and naive thinkers") to the mafia bosses, everything concerning the country is placed under the category of gruesome tastelessness or, as one particularly upset commentator, Dusan I. Bjelic notes, of shit: "Kristeva regards Bulgarians as political excreta, an abject of the polis' superego."[19]

Bulgaria does have, however, one saving grace: In the Middle Ages, it was, in terms of culture and religion, and, as we shall shortly see, in terms of royal marriages, part of the Byzantine civilization. Unlike Bulgaria, Byzantium does figure in Kristeva's writing before the novels bringing up questions of the Eastern Orthodox Church, the father-son relationship, the place of the feminine in Christianity, maternity, medieval and proto-Renaissance painting, and so on. In *Murder in Byzantium* the presence of Bulgaria is purged of its abject "Santa Varvarian" (in the French original it is Santa Barbara, so the B seems to persist) aspects insofar as Bulgarian cultural history is closely intertwined with Byzantium. Bulgarian settings emerge, mostly as enticing landscapes and mysteriously seductive medieval relics, in the context of the novel's quest for the "true story" of the Byzantine princess Anna Comnena. An abject by-product of present-day Santa Varvara, which, since the fall of the Berlin wall, "has expanded continuously,"[20] Bulgaria is also the material holder of traces from a sublime Byzantine past.

The inversion that brings forth a female subject-object dichotomy and a territory bifurcated between abjection and sublimity opens up two theoretically unspeakable realms, which, in Kristeva's novels, seek vent in two distinct styles, the journalistic and the poetic. The first one offers opinions on various issues as directly as can be. It is frequently blunt, self-confident, for the most part unsympathetic and judgmental; it leaves little space for doubt, ambiguity, or, indeed, dialogism and polyphony. It is passionate; it is frankly and openly biased. Sometimes this is the way the characters think; sometimes this is the way they talk: Conversations in Kristeva's novels tend to turn into heated debates. It is worth noting that higher forms of journalism, of the type of *j'accuse*, of the political pamphlet, and of the controversial tract have been set apart as a separate genre in the Russian and Bulgarian literary tradition: It is called *publizistika*, complete with its history dating back to the biblical prophets and Roman satire, with its major representatives and its contemporary researchers. It is opposed to both regular journalism and theory: to the former, through its polemical engagement with ideas rather than events; to the latter, through its emotional appeal to common sense and persuasive power rather than argument. If Stephanie Delacour gave up on the charms of philosophy and sinology and became a reporter, one would assume that it was partially because of the guiles of *publizistika*.

The second realm comprises unique "moments of being" and, in its sensory richness, unpredictability and stunning precision, verges on the impossible. It gives flesh to the singular, thus incorporating the privileged concern of Kristeva's theory as experience rather than as an object of study. The two styles are tied to two divergent novelistic perspectives, one flat, external, and anecdotal; the other one all interiority. They both are free floating in the sense that they can be attached to different characters or speakers in Kristeva's novels. Yet it is also notable that in Kristeva's first novel, *The Samurai*, these two styles are rather evenly distributed between Olga Morena and Joëlle Cabarus, between regular script and italics, and between the social and the intimate. With the next novels they come to coexist in Stephanie Delacour, who, in *Murder in Byzantium*, finds a prototype, a historical precedent in Anna Comnena's capacity to "describe events from the perspective of both a military strategist and a depressed psychologist."[21]

Both styles thus find their native soil, so to speak, in the virtuality of Byzantium. On the one hand, Byzantium is the *publizistika* platform for direct polemical charges against Santa Varvara, as "the opposite of Byzantium,"[22] and as a stand for an alternative vision of Europe. In this aspect it tends to coincide—as a statement but also as a sort of cautionary tale—with contemporary France, this citadel of a dying civilization.[23] On the other hand, Byzantium is the sensuous cipher for the unnamable, a node of utopia and imagination, a different way of seeing and perceiving, a dream and a memory of things that never were, the hope of retrieving a lost territory or, rather, a lost time, a "future anterior."

Under this arch between present and future anterior the recent past, the past that came to be "because of Yalta," once again disappears. Its absence, however, produces a glitch.

ANNA COMNENA AND VERA M.

Anna Comnena's *Alexiad*, which serves as a frame of reference to Kristeva's story about her, is mostly concerned with politics, palace intrigues, military conflicts, and the idealized image of her father, the Byzantine emperor Alexius I. Anna was betrothed for political reasons while still a child; later, for political reasons the betrothal was canceled; she married somebody else and went into no end of effort to have her husband, rather than her younger brother, on the throne; she had several children, four of whom survived; she was ultimately and, in view of her conspiracies, mercifully sent by her imperial brother to a monastery, where she wrote the *Alexiad.* What Kristeva inscribes in this frame is a fictional erotic encounter between Anna and a Western crusader who, as a result of this brief meeting, decides to give up on crusades and marry (not the princess, of course) in Bulgaria. His trajectory is a reversal of Kristeva's own biographical displacement, and there are many marks in the novel indicating the connection.[24] So far as Anna Comnena is concerned, Kristeva's point is that what Anna's writing omits is the one important amorous experience of her life.

The imaginary meeting between Anna Comnena and the knight takes place while Anna is visiting her Bulgarian grandmother: One of the grandmothers of the Byzantine princess was, indeed, a Bulgarian princess. In fact, Kristeva claims in her novel that a Bulgarian historian, "a certain Vera M.,"[25] found proof for this visit about which the *Alexiad* says nothing.

This fleeting intrusion of a contemporary Bulgarian reference deserves unraveling. Vera M. is Vera Mutafchieva, an important historian and novelist whose novel *I, Anna Comnena* appeared for the first time in 1991 and who is also the author of *The Knight*, a novel about a crusader's adventures and death in Bulgaria. *I, Anna Comnena* is of particular interest here. It is structured as alternating narratives in the first person by Anna Comnena and a number of women who were close to her (her mother, her grandmothers, her maid). Unlike Kristeva, who, apart from the fictional love episode, treats Anna Comnena's *Alexiad* with a fair degree of trust, Mutafchieva uses the fictional setting in order to present an entirely different perspective on Anna's biography, on the historical events of the time, on the protagonists in them, and indeed, on the bearing they had on Anna herself. Mutafchieva thus creates a split or, indeed, a chasm between the "official" narrative of the *Alexiad* and the "unofficial" narrative of the female narrators in her novel, a split not simply between the social and the intimate, the political and the personal, the "military strategist" and the "depressed psychologist," but also between political and political, personal and personal, intimate and intimate. It is this chasm that really interests her, the impossibility of really saying "it," the historical truth, or the truth of one's life. What we say or write is not what we think or what happens. Nothing and no one is spared in this undoing of the *Alexiad*, including Anna's idealized father, the Emperor Alexius, about whom Mutafchieva's Anna Comnena dryly notes: "I think my father must have had his spiritual backbone broken very early on in his life and then had grown up with this hidden handicap."[26] There is a brutality, an intellectual ruthlessness in Mutafchieva's effort to make her point, which is in sharp contrast to the dreamy and utopian quality of Kristeva's version with all its dead bodies and indignations against the society of the spectacle. Toward the end of Mutafchieva's novel Anna observes that, for her, the words she writes down in the *Alexiad* have more value and reality than the world of political power, of intrigue and conflicts that she inhabited and described. Yet these words— the *Alexiad*—say nothing about what she knows to be true concerning both the people and the events she writes about, or, indeed, about herself. So why do these words matter to her? And what would be the status of her writing, then? Anna concludes that "writing is not a reflection of being: it is a separate, parallel being. It has its own life, independent of its author."[27]

Mutafchieva's novel reads like a powerful feminist statement: Only, we should add that its strategy of rewriting, with a sharp and merciless eye, of an existing more or less sacrosanct historical and autobiographical account was applied also in other of Mutafchieva's novels where the protagonists were men. Her own father was an eminent "bourgeois" historian, repressed by the communist regime: There is no doubt that her sensitivity to the split between what one writes, what one thinks, and what really takes place provides a wry commentary on the conditions of communist censorship and on her own personal and familial experience. Whatever the case, one year before her death and seventeen years after the first edition of *I, Anna Comnena,* it became known that Mutafchieva was enrolled in 1969 as an informer to the dreaded Sixth Department of the communist secret services, the department spying on and repressing intellectuals.

This knowledge cannot but give a different twist to the chasm Mutafchieva studies in her writing. It uncovers this other, material and quite literal, chasm between her own official writing that got published and the hidden volumes she contributed to the secret services and which must have facilitated the publication of the other ones. So the question that now reads in *I, Anna Comnena*, written immediately after the fall of communism and with Mutafchieva's imminent exposure very likely (it took years, however: another story), runs probably like this: Will my writing stand in spite of its author? With her broken spiritual backbone, with her hidden handicap? Is writing, indeed, a parallel and a better being? To which I would add: Does this writing say what it does not say? Does it instruct us about the survival of thinking under conditions of tyranny? About how, in a story, there is always another story?

Insipid accounts like the one in the award-winning *The Lives of Others*[28] tell us there were good secret agents and humane informers. Surely, there were. Such accounts also try to exonerate intellectuals of the magnitude of playwright Heiner Mueller whose past turned out to be dismally entangled with the secret services. He did no real harm, it was claimed. And yet, the real terror was not about what exactly this or that informer did or did not do. The real terror was the paralysis of thinking that such collaborations were meant to and did incur. And the real question is whether thinking nevertheless took place, through what strategies and at what costs. In her analysis of *Murder in Byzantium*, discussing Kristeva's appeal for Byzantium to be integrated in the European "phantom," Maria Margaroni asks a number of times: What about the communist past of the region? We know: the icons, the Trinity, the crusades, Byzantine culture. What about recent communism? Ultimately, the communist past is not simply about repression and streets less clean but also about tough choices that individuals had to make. It is about the stakes for thought to continue to do its work. If today things with the global Santa Varvara stand as badly as Kristeva believes, the implications of such choices might be the very unsaid that needs the utmost discretion.

Notes

INTRODUCTION

1. Hannah Arendt, *Between Past and Future: Eight Exercises in Political Thought* (Harmondsworth, Eng.: Penguin Books, 1977), 5–6.

2. Tzotcho Boiadjiev, "Predgovor" [Introduction] to *Filosofski Seminari: Gjolechitsa—20 Godini* [Philosophical Seminars: 20 Years After] (Sofia: Minerva, 2004), 9. Unless otherwise stated, all translations are by the author.

3. I provide more details about this growing literature in Chapter 1.

4. Alain Badiou, *Infinite Thought: Truth and the Return to Philosophy*, trans. and ed. Oliver Feltham and Justin Clemens (London: Continuum, 2005), 101.

5. See Ellen Rooney, "A Semiprivate Room," *Differences: A Journal of Feminist Cultural Studies* 13, no. 1 (2002): 128–56.

6. Tzotcho Boiadjiev, "Dialogichnijat printsip na istoriko-kulturnoto isledvane" [The Dialogical Principle of Historic Cultural Research], in *Avgustin i Dekart* [St. Augustine and Descartes] (Sofia: Sofia University Press, 1992).

7. Tzvetan Stoyanov, "Za hubavite razgovori" [On Good Conversations]. *Kulturata kato obshtenie* [Culture as Communication] (Sofia: Bulgarski pisatel, 1988), 68–69.

8. Tzotcho Boiadjiev, *"Nepisanoto uchenie" na Platon* [Plato's Unwritten Doctrine] (Sofia: Nauka i izkustvo, 1984), 20–21. The insistence on avoiding the lures of "mystical silence" contains a long story that I cannot really give here. Boiadjiev's point is that, if writing ran the risk of being suppressed by censorship, mystical silence—which had come into vogue through the eccentric New Age allegiances of the dictator's daughter who died under mysterious circumstances at the beginning of the 1980s—simply did nothing.

9. Boiadjiev, "Dialogichnijat printsip," 112.

10. Stoyanov, "On Good Conversations," 69.

11. Boyan Manchev, "Interpretatsii na ideologiata ideologia na interpretatsiata: Vîrhu polemikite v bîlgarskoto literaturoznanie" [Interpretation of Ideology, Ideologies of Interpretation: On the Debates in Bulgarian Literary Theory], *Literaturna misîl* 1 (1999): 5–30.

12. Tzotcho Boiadjiev, "Marsilio Ficino ili Eros kato krîgovrat na duha" [Marsilio Ficino or Eros as *Circuitus Spiritualis*], in *Krîgovrat na duha* (Sofia: LiK, 1998), 195.

13. Alexander Kiossev, "Paranoia de la parrhesia," in *Michel Foucault: Les jeux de la verité et du pouvoir: Etudes transeuropéennes,* ed. Alain Brossat (Nancy: Presses Universitaires de Nancy, 1994).

14. Slavoj Žižek, *The Parallax View* (Cambridge, Mass.: MIT Press, 2006), 4.

15. I discuss this in Chapter 3.

16. It is worth noting that Russian (like Bulgarian and other Slavic languages) has a word for "human being" (*chelovek*) that differs from the words for man (*muzhchina*) and woman (*zhenshchina*). Former uses in English (or French) of the word "man" as "human being" would always appear as *chelovek* in Russian: This is the word Merab Mamardashvili employs in the texts of his that I discuss later on. Wherever in the book I use "man" rather than "human being" I do it in order to emphasize the historical dimension of the debate.

17. Joan Scott, "Fictitious Unities: 'Gender,' 'East' and 'West,'" Fourth Feminist Research Conference, Bologna, September 2000. http://www.women.it/cyberarchive/files/scott.htm.

18. Wendy Brown, *Edgework: Critical Essays on Knowledge and Politics* (Princeton: Princeton University Press, 2005), 99.

19. Ibid., 114.

1. THE SEMINAR: *MODE D'EMPLOI:* IMPURE SPACES IN THE LIGHT OF LATE TOTALITARIANISM

1. "After November 10 the fossils [of the seminar] were uncovered in the basement of the Sofia University" (Ani Ilkov, *Izvorît na groznohubavite* [The Fountain of the Ugly Beauties] [Sofia: Anubis, 1994], 11). Although many texts were written in the 1980s, few were published during that time, and the seminar was, for reasons of censorship, a mostly oral occurrence. Most of the publications and the controversies took place in book collections and in the press in the 1990s, with some major clashes occurring between "dark blue" and "light blue" opposition to communism, between "postmodernists" and "medievalists," and another one around feminism (no one proclaimed themselves antifeminist in this debate, but men systematically tended to forget about women in their account of the events). Part of this ultimately rather bulky writing spilled over into other languages at about the same time in the 1990s (Alexander Kiossev, ed., *Post-Theory, Games, and Discursive Resistance: The Bulgarian Case* [Albany: State University of New York Press, 1995]; Vladislav Todorov, *Red Square/Black Square: Organon for Revolutionary Imagination* [Albany: State University of New York Press, 1995]; Ivan Stanev, *Lapsus Linguae: Theaterstücke, Theoretische Lähmungen, Ontologische Gesänge* [Berlin: Autoren Kollegium, 1992]). These books exemplify both what the seminar produced at its most extreme and how it functioned. A tamer echo from the earlier years resulted from a rather consternating encounter between the seminar and the "West" that, from a fantasmatic counterpart (I will return to this in the next chapter), materialized as a group of leading Foucault scholars who came to a conference in Sofia in 1993. There was a scandal or, to use Kiossev's phrase, a "big misunderstanding": political but also academic. Nevertheless, a collection did come out of it (Alain Brossat, ed., *Michel Foucault: Les jeux de la verité et du pouvoir: Etudes transeuropéennes* [Nancy: Presses Universitaires de Nancy, 1994]). The number of publications in Bulgarian that came directly out of the seminar's auditoriums is hard to estimate. The most extensive studies, both in Bulgarian and in other languages, focus on *Ecoglasnost*, that is, the final stage when the "seminar" was transformed into a political movement (Bernd Baumgartl, *Transition and Sustainability: Actors and Interests in Eastern European Environmental Policies*

[Boston: Kluwer Law International, 1997]). After the changes, two weekly magazines, *Literaturen vestnik* and *Kultura*, and the journal *Kritika i humanizîm*, provided a sort of continuation for the seminar but already in the new situation of stratification and fragmentation of the aesthetic, theoretical, and political positions.

2. Gorbachev's term "glasnost" comes from the old Slavonic root for "voice" (*glas*), whose form and meaning have been preserved in Bulgarian. In Russian, the word has an archaic flavor and might take us to nineteenth-century resistance to tsarism or, as I will do toward the end of this essay, to Bakhtin's privileging of the irreducible multiplicity of the *phonē*.

3. "Factories are not built to produce commodities. . . . They are allegorical figures of industrialization. Industry represents the leading metaphor of party ideology and factories are the works of this ideology. They result in a deficit of goods, but in overproduction of symbolic meanings." Etc. (Todorov, *Red Square/Black Square,* 10.)

4. Joan W. Scott, *Only Paradoxes to Offer: French Feminists and the Rights of Man* (Cambridge, Mass.: Harvard University Press, 1996).

5. Steven Goldsmith, "The Textual Logic of Democracy: Theory and the Crisis of Representation," in *The Ends of Theory*, ed. Jerry Herron, Dorothy Huson, Ross Pudaloff, and Robert Strozier (Detroit: Wayne State University Press, 1996), 139.

6. Angel Angelov, "Dialog i dialogizm" [Dialogue and Dialogism], *Literaturen vestnik,* 9 April 1997.

7. There was also a feminist method described in my text: the "method of flinging the book," with Martin Luther and Virginia Woolf as its venerable predecessors (they fling an inkpot at other things, but never mind). An indication that I had struck some communal seminar feeling was the fact that in 1989 I was invited to "tour" a number of different seminars with this text and that immediately after the changes between 1990 and 1992 it was published three times (Miglena Nikolchina, "Postmodernata biblioteka" [The Postmodern Library], in *I prochee* [Etcetera], ed. M. Abigar, V. Miteva, and H. Todorov [Sofia: Sofia University Press, 1990], 95–105).

8. An emblematic title for this agenda, simultaneously hidden and self-evident, would be Kolyo Koev, "The Invisible Horizons of the Self-Evident," *Abstracts of the Eighth International Congress of Logic, Methodology and Philosophy of Science* (Moscow, 1987), vol. 5, pt. 2, 394–96.

9. This tradition, the major Bulgarian proponents of which from the 1960s on have been Nikola Georgiev and Radosvet Kolarov, was related to the Russian formalists, the Prague linguistic circle, R. Jakobson, M. Bakhtin, Y. Lotman, and others. At the beginning of the 1970s the International Association for Semiotic Studies (founded in 1969) included three Bulgarians in its thirty-member executive committee (Boyan Manchev, "Interpretatsii na ideologiata, ideologia na interpretatsiata: Vîrhu polemikite v bîlgarskoto literaturoznanie" [Interpretation of Ideology, Ideologies of Interpretation: On the Debates in Bulgarian Literary Theory], *Literaturna misîl* 1 (1999): n. 32). The Sofia University graduates Tzvetan Todorov and Julia Kristeva, who, in the 1960s in France, acted as mediators for the Western reception of this tradition, became in the 1980s emblematic figures for the reverse "traffic" of new developments in Western theory toward us.

10. This was a long year, though. Peter Manolov, for example, was forced, through threats concerning his son's life, to leave the country.

11. Alexander Kiossev, "Golyamoto nedorazumenie: Zapad i iztok, paresiasti, filosofi, polititsi i medii v ikonomikata na istinata" [The Big Misunderstanding: West, East, Parrhesiasts, Philosophers, Politicians, and the Media in the Economy of Truth], in *Medii i mitove* [Media and Myths], ed. Georgi Lozanov and Orlin Spasov, 17–97. Sofia: Sofia University Press, 2000.

12. Michel Foucault, *Fearless Speech* (Los Angeles: Semiotext(e), 2001).

13. Vaclav Havel, *The Power of the Powerless: Citizens against the State in Central-Eastern Europe*, ed. John Keane (New York: M. E. Sharpe, 1985), 39.

14. Alexander Kiossev, "Introduction: A Broken Promise," in *Post-Theory, Games, and Discursive Resistance: The Bulgarian Case*, ed. Alexander Kiossev (Albany: State University of New York Press, 1995), xvii.

15. Jean-Pierre Vernant, "Mamardashvili, chovekîit na slovoto" [Mamardashvili, the Man of the Word], *Kultura,* 1 December 2000.

16. Deyan Deyanov, "Filosofskoto inakomislie na Mamardashvili" [The Philosophical *Inakomislie* of Mamardashvili], *Kritika i humanizîm* 6 (1999): 6.

17. Deyan Deyanov, "Neklasicheskata ratsionalnost kato problemno pole" [Nonclassical Rationality as a Problem Field], *Kritika i humanizîm* 6 (1999): 5–6.

18. Deyanov, "Filosofskoto," 6.

19. Andrei Raichev, "Migratsionnite obshtestva i vtorata mrezha" [The Migration Societies and the Second Network], *Kritika i humanizîm* 3 (1991): 198.

20. "I don't know what feminism is, but I say NO," "Why I Am Not a Feminist," "Why Is There No Feminism after Communism" are titles that sum up the trend immediately after the fall of communism (Laura Busheikin, Mira Marody, Jeffrey C. Goldfarb). On the one hand, it was that "we had enough of this emancipation scrap during communism." On the other hand, feminism was perceived as on a par with McDonald's and Coca Cola (Jirina Siklova, "McDonalds, Terminators, Coca Cola Ads, and Feminism?" in *Bodies of Bread and Butter: Reconfiguring Women's Lives in Post-Communist Czech Republic*, ed. Susana Trnka and Laura Busheikin [Prague: Prague Gender Center, 1993], 7–11). The third type of response was summarized in private conversation by the daughter of an ad hoc activist as "I am your feminist; where is the money?" The result was that, in the situation of the drastic impoverishment of East European academia during the 1990s, Western funding consistently preferred the more compliant NGOs to an academy that remained critical to imposed priorities.

21. Hana Havelkova, "Transitory and Persistent Differences: Feminism East and West," in *Transitions, Environments, Translations: Feminism in International Politics*, ed. Joan Scott, Cora Kaplan, and Debra Keates (New York: Routledge, 1997), 56–62; Mira Marody, "Why I Am Not a Feminist: Some Remarks on the Problem of Gender Identity in the United States and Poland," *Social Research: An International Quarterly of the Social Sciences* 60, no. 4 (1993): 853–64; Jirina Siklova, "Feminism and the Roots of Apathy in the Czech Republic," *Social Research: An International Quarterly of the Social Sciences* 64, no. 2 (1997): 258–80.

22. Joanne P. Sharp, "Gendering Nationhood: A Feminist Engagement with National Identity," in *Body Space: Destabilizing Geographies of Gender and Sexuality*, ed. Nancy Duncan (New York: Routledge, 1996), 102.

23. In "The Family: How to Use It" the Bulgarian theoretician Nicola Georgiev examines the consecutive ideological shifts in the treatment of gender differences (similar shifts were a common feature of many of the communist countries) in conjunction with the

history of the family of Todor Zhivkov, who ruled Bulgaria for more than thirty years. Far from either idealizing or underestimating the "uses" of the family, which was the focus of ever new strategies of control, Georgiev lays bare the manipulative efforts exerted by the repressive ideological machine precisely in the arena of gender. The state-orchestrated shift from "revolutionary" to more traditional gender patterns is thus seen not as a simple and altogether benign softening of the regime or, alternatively, as a popular victory that allowed age-old mores to reappear but as a strategy that consolidated the power of the dictator bringing into use his own family cum phallic mother, effaced wife, and daughter communicating with the powers that be.

24. Renata Salecl, *The Spoils of Freedom: Psychonalaysis and Feminism after the Fall of Socialism* (New York: Rougledge, 1994), 3.

25. Andrej Bundzhulov, *Heterotopii* (Sofia: Kritika i humanizîm, 1995); "Modernoto obshtestvo i socialisticheskata heterotopia" [Modern Society and the Socialist Heterotopia], *Kritika i humanizîm* 3 (1991): 207–23; "Vlast i vidimost: Uvod vîv fenomenologiata na heliotorpizmite" [Power and Visibility: An Introduction to the Phenomenology of Heliotropisms], *Kritika i humanizîm* 6 (1999): 161–76.

26. Peggy Watson, "Rethinking Transition: Globalism, Gender, and Class," *International Feminist Journal of Politics* 2, no. 2 (2000): 185–213.

27. Peggy Watson, "Civil Society and the Politics of Difference in Eastern Europe," in *Transitions, Environments, Translations: Feminism in International Politics,* ed. Joan Scott, Cora Kaplan, and Debra Keates (New York: Routledge, 1997), 25.

28. Todorov, *Red Square/Black Square,* 4. Renata Salecl's insistence on the distinction between the "dead father" (empty space of authority) of democracy and the "obscene father" as the authoritarian leader (*The Spoils of Freedom,* 99–101) can provide the basis for a distinction between the regime in former Yugoslavia (with its obscene fathers) and the regimes in the Soviet bloc proper where the dead and the obscene father collapsed into a corpse—Lenin's mummy.

29. "Mummacrum" is the "mummy simulacrum." A reminder is perhaps necessary that the mummy of Lenin did take center stage in the quasi public space (Todorov, *Red Square/Black Square,*135 and passim).

30. Havel, *Power of the Powerless,* 25.

31. Vladislav Todorov, "Teror i terorizîm" [Terror and Terrorism], in *Medii i mitove* [Media and Myths], ed. Georgi Lozanov and Orlin Spasov (Sofia: Sofia University Press, 2000), 250–59.

32. The ambiguity of private and public was a recurring preoccupation of the seminar (Nina Nikolova, "Politanatomiya na moderniya chovek" [Political Anatomy of the Modern Human Being], *Kritika i humanizîm* 3 [1991]: 91–109; Svetlana Subeva, "Kîm kriticheskata istoriya na modernata publichnost" [Toward the Critical History of Modern Publicity], *Kritika i humanizîm* 3 [1991]: 111–22).

33. Raichev, "Migratsionnite."

34. It had its language, of course, the language of cynical duplicity. This was the language that the drivers of the comrades used while waiting, the language that the journalists in the big communist dailies used after work, the language that the agents in the Sixth Department (the one dealing with intellectuals) used among themselves, the language that everybody used in order to let off steam and go on living. This language survived the regime and played a disastrous role during the transition (Lilyana Deyanova, "Nevîzmozhnata kriticheska publichnost" [The Impossible Critical Publicity], in *Medii i prehod* [Media and Transition], ed. Georgi Lozanov, Lilyana Deyanova, and Orlin Spasov [Sofia: Center for Media Development, 2000], 240–56).

35. Julian Popov, "'Za nas kinoto e nai-vazhnoto izkustvo'" [For Us Cinema Is the Most Important Art], in *Ars Erotica*, ed. Orlin Spasov, 172–76. Sofia: Institute for Children's Literature and Art, 1992.

36. Todorov, *Red Square/Black Square,* 83.

37. Popov, "Za nas kinoto," 174. As one of the last 1980s jokes, the rather obscene collection on the "erotics of communism" where Popov's text appeared was published by the Sofia Institute for Children's Arts and Literature.

38. Popov, "'Za nas kinoto,'" 174.

39. Qtd. in Todorov, *Red Square/Black Square,* 82.

40. Ivaylo Ditchev, "Erotika na komunizma" [The Erotic of Communism], in *Ars Erotica*, ed. Orlin Spasov (Sofia: Institute for Children's Literature and Art, 1992), 156–57.

41. On the coded and normative "stylized" eroticism of the workplace in Russia (which, I believe, is applicable to other former communist countries) see Elena Zdravomyslova and Anna Temkina, "Social'noe konstruktirovanie gendera kak feministkaya teoriya"

[The Social Construction of Gender as Feminist Theory], in *Zhenshchina, gender, kultura* [Woman, Gender, and Culture], 61–62 (Moscow: MZGI, 1999).

42. Ivaylo Ditchev, "Literalisms," in *Post-Theory, Games, and Discursive Resistance: The Bulgarian Case,* by Alexander Kiossev et al. (Albany: State University of New York Press, 1995), 3–9.

43. Vladislav Todorov, "Eros, Ritsariat na protezata" [Eros, the Knight of the Prosthesis], in *Ars Erotica*, ed. Orlin Spasov (Sofia: Institute for Children's Literature and Art, 1992), 219–53; Boryana Katsarska, "Dusha. Eros. Obshtnost" [Soul. Eros. Community], *Filosofski pregled* 2, no. 2 (1992): 3–14; Kalin Yanakiev, "Vsekidnevniyat svyat na srednovekovniya chovek: Eros i distantsiya" [The Everyday Life of the Medieval Person: Eros and Distance], in *Ars Erotica*, ed. Orlin Spasov (Sofia: Institute for Children's Literature and Art, 1992), 19–33.

44. Albena Stambolova, "Pisane i prelîstyavane" [Writing and Seduction], in *Ars Erotica*, ed. Orlin Spasov (Sofia: Institute for Children's Literature and Art, 1992), 60–65; Jana Damyanova, "Protsesît na samotniya prelîstitel ili stradanieto na pisatelya ot podzemieto" [The Process/Trial of the Solitary Seducer; or, the Suffering of the Writer from the Underground], in *Ars Erotica*, ed. Orlin Spasov (Sofia: Institute for Children's Literature and Art, 1992), 66–88.

45. Krasimira Krushkova, "Ustnite kato kavichki" [The Lips as Quotation Marks], in *Ars Erotica*, ed. Orlin Spasov (Sofia: Institute for Children's Literature and Art, 1992), 95.

46. As Alexander Kiossev put it in one of the short-lived periodicals after the changes, "A spiritual community emerges only between two and only between men" (qtd. in Amelia Licheva, "Golyamoto mîzhko priyatelstvo ili ima li neshto obshto mezhdu Robinzon Kruzo, Herman Hese i Aleksandîr Kyosev" [Sublime Male Bonding, or What Does Alexander Kiossev Have in Common with Robinson Crusoe and Herman Hesse], *Kultura,* 10 July 1992). After such a statement, the (possible) relegation of women's participation to the "spouses and friends" mentioned in Kiossev's Introduction to *Post-Theory* (xvii) looks like a positive development.

47. Women were much better represented in the "classicist" and "young Marxian" journals and collections than in the "postmodernist" ones. The exploration of this paradox, given the celebrated poststructuralist interest in "difference," would, I believe, ultimately take us to questions of time and genealogy. Women are perceived as

a threat not in spatial terms but insofar as they disrupt male filiations. Postmodernist perspectives have been the only ones so far to present such disruption as a serious theoretical possibility: Hence they are more wary of women's input. And yet, as Joan Scott has demonstrated in "Fantasy Echo," being a woman does not warrant a way out from this structural fix. I treat these issues in *Matricide.*

48. Peggy Watson, "The Rise of Masculinism in Eastern Europe," *New Left Review* 198 (1993): 71–82; Joan W. Scott, "Fictitious Unities: 'Gender,' 'East' and 'West,' " Fourth Feminist Research Conference, Bologna, September 2000, http://www.women.it/cyberarchive/files/scott.htm.

49. The written and unwritten trajectories that studied and discussed the problem of everyday life against the grain of the official ideology—largely through the efforts of sociologist Kolio Koev, among others—form a separate chapter in the activities of the seminar. See Simona Treneva, "Za edna alternative na ofitsialnata bulgarska sotsiologia v kraia na 70te i prez 80te godini na 20 vek" [Toward an Alternative of the Official Bulgarian Sociology from the End of the 1970s and during the 1980s], *Sotsiologicheski problemi* 37, no. 3–4 (2005): 296–99.

50. Bundzhulov, *Heterotopii*; "Modernoto obshtestvo;" "Vlast i vidimost."

51. Michel Foucault, "Of Other Spaces," *Diacritics* 16, no. 1 (1986): 24.

52. Nancy Fraser, *Justice Interruptus: Critical Reflections on the "Postsocialist" Condition* (New York: Routledge, 1997), 3.

2. THE WEST AS INTELLECTUAL UTOPIA

1. Susan Buck-Morss, *Dreamworld and Catastrophe: The Passing of Mass Utopia in East and West* (Cambridge, Mass.: MIT Press, 2000), 238–39.

2. Yuri Lotman, *Kul'tura i vzryv* [Culture and Explosion] (Moscow: Gnozis, 1992), 96.

3. Yuri Lotman, "Sovremennost mezhdu Vostokom i Zapadom" [The Present between East and West], *Znamia,* no. 9 (1997): 162.

4. Michel Foucault, "Of Other Spaces," *Diacritics* 16, no. 1 (1986): 24.

5. Ibid., 23.

6. Gianni Vattimo, *The Transparent Society,* trans. David Webb (Cambridge: Polity Press, 1992), 73.

7. Mikhail Ryklin, "Parnikovyi effect" [The Greenhouse Effect]. 1994. http://azbuka.gif.ru/critics/parnik/.

8. Michel Foucault, "Les heterotopias," in *Die Heterotopien: Les heterotopias. Der utopische Körper. Le corps utopique* (Frankfurt am Main: Suhrkamp, 2005), 50–51.

9. Frances Stonor Saunders, "Modern Art Was CIA 'Weapon': Revealed: How the Spy Agency Used Unwitting Artists such as Pollock and de Kooning in a Cultural Cold War," *Independent,* 22 October 1995.

10. Buck-Morss. *Dreamworld and Catastrophe,* 237, 331n35.

11. Ryklin, "Parnikovyi."

12. Ibid.

13. Elena Petrovskaia, "Jetot smutnyj obraz devjanostyh" [The Murky Image of the Nineties], *Hudozhestvennyj Zhurnal,* no. 25 (1999): 14.

14. Ibid., 13.

15. Susan Buck-Morss, "Pis'mo iz Nyu-Iorka" [A Letter from New York], *Hudozhestvennyi zhurnal,* no. 25 (1999): 18.

16. Fredric Jameson, "Conversations on the New World Order," in *After the Fall: The Failure of Communism and the Future of Socialism,* ed. Robin Blackburn (New York: Verso, 1991), 260, 265. Here is Buck-Morss's comment: "Although Jameson does not mention the Dubrovnik meeting specifically, it is clearly the experience he has in mind when he speaks of 'Yugoslavia, Bulgaria and the Soviet Union' in this essay written in March 1991, five months after our meeting" (*Dreamworld and Catastrophe,* 331n36).

17. Lotman, *Kul'tura,* 25.

18. Wendy Brown, *States of Injury: Power and Freedom in Late Modernity* (Princeton: Princeton University Press, 1995), 7.

19. Ibid., 26.

20. Wendy Brown, *Politics Out of History* (Princeton: Princeton University Press, 2001), 13.

21. Slavoj Žižek, "A Plea for Leninist Intolerance," *Critical Inquiry* vol. 28, no. 2 (2002): 543.

22. Buck-Morss, *Dreamworld and Catastrophe,* 243.

23. Merab Mamardashvili, *Lektsii po antichnoi filosofii* [Lectures in Ancient Greek Philosophy] (Moscow: Agraf, 1997), 8.

24. Nancy Fraser, *Justice Interruptus: Critical Reflections on the "Postsocialist" Condition* (New York: Routledge, 1997), 3.

25. Vladimir Vernadsky, "Neskol'ko lov o noosfere" [A Few Words about the Noosphere], in *Russkii kosmizm: Antologia filosofskoi mysli*, ed. A. G. Gacheva and S. G. Semyonova (Moscow: Pedagogika-Press, 1993), 309.

26. Michael Holquist, "Tsiolkovsky as a Moment in the Prehistory of the Avant-Garde," in *Laboratory of Dreams: The Russian Avant-Garde and Cultural Experiment*, ed. J. E. Bowlt and O. Matich (Stanford: Stanford University Press, 1996), 100–117; Vladislav Todorov, "The Conquest of the Vacuum" (manuscript; no date).

27. Victor H. Lawn, "Satellite Rivals Sirius over City: New Yorkers Note Brilliance as They Get First View of an Artificial Moon." *New York Times*, 8 November 1957. Available at http://www.nytimes.com/partners/aol/special/sputnik/sput-19.html.

28. Hannah Arendt, *The Human Condition* (Chicago: University of Chicago Press, 1958), 1.

29. Vladislav Todorov, *Red Square/Black Square: Organon for Revolutionary Imagination* (Albany: State University of New York Press, 1995), 65–66.

30. Ivaylo Ditchev, *Donner sans perdre: L'échange dans l'imaginaire de la modernité* (Paris: Harmattan, 1997), 74.

31. Ibid., 91.

32. Dimitrina Petrova, "Bulgaria," in *Dissent and Opposition in Communist Eastern Europe: Origins of Civil Society and Democratic Transition*, ed. D. Pollack and J. W. Aldershot (London: Ashgate, 2004), 180.

33. Here is Petrova's story about what happened after she was summoned for an interview with the Sixth Department: "Krassimir Kanev then helped me think up a strategy of behavior toward the 'organs,' based on the following assumptions. Firstly, the 'organs' had no sufficient technological surveillance capacity to monitor and document dissenting statements, and the student informers had probably provided oral and/or written reports but no tape-recorded evidence of my statements. Secondly, security officials were not as competent on Marxist ideology as the regime's critics, who had studied it most scrupulously. Thirdly, security officials relied on strictly individual intimidation, and wanted to avoid, by all means, spreading the fact that they were trying to intimidate university professors one

by one. Last but not least, at this point in time, unlike during earlier times, the 'organs' were no longer prepared to kill or torture opponents of the regime, especially if the latter belonged in intellectual circles of the capital Sofia. All these assumptions were correct. Accused of neo-Hegelianism, I argued with my interrogator on the subtleties of neo-Hegelian ideas, of which, as it turns out, the interrogator knew very little. Pressured to sign a warning that the meeting and its contents must not be revealed, since they constituted 'classified information,' I simply refused to sign. Moreover, I declared that the following day I would tell the story of having been interrogated at the faculty meeting to as many colleagues as possible. (Which, as a matter of fact, is precisely what I did.) The main lessons that could be learned from this and similar episodes, and the strategy that could thus be devised in dealing with such an interrogation situation spread quickly. Broad publicity in the unofficial public sphere had a protective function. Moreover, security officers were unable to keep up once the discourse embarked upon intellectual and ideological waters. Thus, anything uttered before security officials should be strictly limited to abstract ideas, whereas complete silence should be observed on concrete facts and especially on individual people. Furthermore, despite all of the above, it would be best to simply refuse any communication whatsoever, since the work of the intellectual police (Sixth Department of the Committee on State Security) was illegal anyway" ("Bulgaria," 182).

34. Anesa Miller-Pogacar, "Introduction: Mikhail Epstein's Transcultural Visions," in *After the Future: The Paradoxes of Postmodernism and Contemporary Russian Culture,* by Mikhail N. Epstein (Amherst: University of Massachusetts Press, 1995), 4.

35. Buck-Morss, *Dreamworld and Catastrophe*, 223.

36. "The high prestige of mathematics and theoretical physics (prized by the Soviet establishment for ideological reasons as the pinnacle of materialist science and for practical reasons as the key to technological success) smoothed the way for discussion of humanistic themes that combined references to quantum mechanics and linguistic models" (Laura Engelstein, "Culture, Culture Everywhere: Interpretations of Modern Russia, across the 1991 Divide," *Kritika: Explorations in Russian and Eurasian History* 2, no. 2 [2001]: 387).

37. Stanislaw Lem, *Microworlds*, ed. Franz Rottensteiner (San Diego: Harcourt Brace Jovanovich, 1984), 205–6.

38. Ibid., 106.

39. For three diverse perspectives on Philip K. Dick's letters to the FBI see Heer, "Marxist Critics are Following Me!"; Philmus, "The Two Faces of Philip K. Dick"; Rickman, "Dick, Deception, and Dissociation."

40. P. A. Florensky, "Perepiska" [Letters], *Novyi mir,* no. 2 (1989): 197.

41. Yuri Lotman, *Universe of the Mind: A Semiotic Theory of Culture,* trans. A. Shukman (London: Tauris, 1990), 150.

42. Andrej Bunzhulov, *Heterotopii* (Sofia: Kritika i humanizîm, 1995), 19.

43. Jorge Luis Borges, "Tlön, Uqbar, Orbis Tertius," in *Labyrinths: Selected Stories and Other Writings,* ed. Donald A. Yates and James E. Irby (New York: New Directions, 1964), 3.

44. Ibid., 4.

3. BETWEEN IRONY AND REVOLUTION: SEXUAL DIFFERENCE AND THE CASE OF *AUFHEBUNG*

1. Jacques Derrida, "From Restricted to General Economy: A Hegelianism without Reserve," in *Writing and Difference,* trans. Alan Bass (Chicago: University of Chicago Press, 1978), 257.

2. A. I. Volodin, *Gegel' i russkaja socialisticheskaja mysl' XIX veka* [Hegel and Russian Nineteenth-Century Socialist Thinking] (Moscow: Mysl', 1973), 6.

3. Oleg Sumin, *Gegel' kak sud'ba Rossii* [Hegel as the Destiny of Russia] (Sofia: Malvina, 1997).

4. Ibid., 43.

5. Volodin, *Gegel' i russkaja socialisticheskaja mysl',* 8, 235.

6. G. W. F. Hegel, *Sochinenija* (Moscow-Leningrad, 1934). 7: xv.

7. Sumin, *Gegel' kak sud'ba Rossii,* 90.

8. V. I. Lenin, "Gosudarstvo i revoljucija: Uchenie marksizma o gosudarstve i zadachi proletariata v revoljucii," in *Polnoe sobranie sochinenij,* 5-e izd., vol. 33 (Moscow: Izdatel'stvo politicheskoj literatury, 1969), 70.

9. V. I. Lenin, "Filosofskie tetrady," in *Polnoe sobranie, sochinenij,* 5-e izd., vol. 29 (Moscow: Izdatel'stvo politicheskoj literatury, 1969), 330.

10. Ibid., 92.

11. Jacques Derrida, "Qu'est-ce qu'une traduction 'relevante'?" in *Jacques Derrida,* ed. Marie-Louise Mallet and Ginette Michaud (Paris: Éditions de l'Herne, 2004), 561–76.

12. Gwendoline Jarczyk and Perre-Jean Labarrière, "Sursumer/ Sursomption," in *Hegeliana* (Paris: Presses Universitaire de France, 1986), 102–20.

13. Jean-Luc Nancy, *La remarque spéculative (un bon mot de Hegel)* (Paris: Galilée, 1973), 18n4.

14. Alexandre Kojève, *Introduction à la lecture de Hegel* (Paris: Gallimard, 1947), 482.

15. Jean Wahl, "Le role de A. Koyré dans le developpement des études hegeliennes en France," *Hegel-Studien*, Beiheft, 3 (1966): 22.

16. Jacques Derrida, "Différance," in *Margins of Philosophy*, trans. Alan Bass (Chicago: University of Chicago Press, 1982), 13.

17. Jacques Derrida, *Positions*, trans. Alan Bass (Chicago: University of Chicago Press, 1981), 44.

18. Michael Inwood, *A Hegel Dictionary* (Oxford: Blackwell, 2003), 284.

19. Derrida, "Différance," 20, trans. n. 23.

20. Jarczyk and Labarrière, "Sursumer/Sursomption," 110.

21. For example, in Victor Delbos, "Les Facteurs kantiens dans la philosophie allemande," *Revue de Métaphysique et de Morale* 23 (1925): 271–81. See Alexandre Koyré, "Rapport sur l'état des études hégeliennes en France," in *Études d'histoire de la pensée philosophique* (Paris: Gallimard, 1971), 235n1.

22. Koyré, "Rapport sur l'état des études hégeliennes en France," 213, 215.

23. Alexandre Koyré, "Hegel à Iéna," in *Études d'histoire de la pensée philosophique* (Paris: Gallimard, 1971), 161.

24. Alexandre Koyré, "Note sur la langue et la terminologie hégelienne," in *Études d'histoire de la pensée philosophique* (Paris: Gallimard, 1971), 209.

25. Kojève, *Introduction à la lecture de Hegel*, 21.

26. Derrida, "Qu'est-ce qu'une traduction 'relevante'?" 573.

27. Jacques Lacan, "L'étourdit," in *Autres écrits* (Paris: Le Seuil, 2001), 453.

28. Jacques Lacan, "The Signification of the Phallus," in *Feminine Sexuality: Jacques Lacan and the école freudienne*, ed. Juliet Mitchell and Jacqueline Rose (New York: Norton, 1985), 82.

Here goes the French version: "signe lui-même de la latence dont est frappé tout signifiable, dès lors qu'il est élevé (*aufgehoben*) à la fonction de signifiant. Le phallus est le signifiant de cette *Aufhebung* elle-même inaugure (initie) par sa disparition" (Jacques Lacan, *Écrits II* [Paris: Seuil, 1999], 70).

29. Jacques Lacan, *Seminaire livre* XX (Paris: Seuil, 1975), 79.

30. Alain Badiou, *Theory of the Subject*, trans. Bruno Bosteels (London: Continuum, 2009), 170.

31. V. I. Lenin, "Detskaja bolezn' 'levizny' v kommunizme," *Polnoe sobranie*, vol. 41 (Moscow: Izdatel'stvo politicheskoj literatury, 1981), 69–70.

32. See also Judith Butler, *Bodies That Matter: On the Discursive Limits of "Sex"* (New York: Routledge, 1993), and *Undoing Gender* (New York: Routledge, 2004).

33. Butler, *Bodies That Matter*, 95.

34. Joan Copjec, "Sex and the Euthanasia of Reason," in *Read My Desire: Lacan against the Historicists* (Cambridge, Mass.: MIT Press, 1995), 201.

35. Ibid., 236.

36. Ibid.

37. Ibid., 234.

38. Joan Rivière, "Womanliness as a Masquerade," in *Formations of Fantasy*, ed. Victor Burgin, James Donald and Cora Kaplan (New York: Methuen, 1986), 35–44.

39. Badiou, *Theory of the Subject*, 262.

40. Wendy Brown, *Edgework: Critical Essays on Knowledge and Politics* (Princeton: Princeton University Press, 2005), 99.

41. Slavoj Žižek, *The Parallax View* (Cambridge, Mass.: MIT Press, 2006), 4.

42. Seyla Benhabib, *Situating the Self: Gender, Community, and Postmodernism in Contemporary Ethics* (New York: Routledge, 1992), 256.

43. Alenka Zupančič, *The Odd One In: On Comedy* (Cambridge, Mass.: MIT Press, 2008), 178.

44. Badiou, *Theory of the Subject*, 144.

45. Giorgio Agamben, *The Time That Remains: A Commentary on the Letter to the Romans*, trans. Patricia Dailey (Stanford: Stanford University Press, 2005), 95–101.

46. Merab Mamardashvili, *Kantianskiye variatsii* [Kantian Variations] (Moscow: Agraf, 2002), 25.

47. Catharine Malabou, *La plasticité au soir de l'écriture: Dialectique, destruction, deconstruction* (Paris: Léo Scheer, 2005), 68.

4. AN UNFINISHED PROJECT: MAN AS COMEDY

1. Simone de Beauvoir, *The Second Sex,* trans. H. M. Parshley (New York: Everyman's Library, 1993), 281.

2. Ibid., 35. See, however, Judith Butler, "Sex and Gender in Simone de Beauvoir's *Second Sex*," *Yale French Studies* 72 (1986): 35–49. Later on, in *Gender Trouble: Feminism and the Subversion of Identity* (New York: Routledge, 1990), Butler revokes some of her earlier statements on Beauvoir, which nevertheless strike me as more true to the spirit of *The Second Sex* and which, it seems to me, have played a seminal role in the evolution of Butler's own theoretical stance.

3. Merab Mamardashvili, "Evropeyskaya otvetstvennost'" [The European Responsibility], in *Soznaniye i tsivilizatsiya* (Moscow: Logos, 2004), 27–28.

4. "I believe that European culture contains, if you wish, the only acceptable answer to the question whether change is still possible in the world" (ibid., 28). Let me note once again that Mamardashvili had not been allowed to leave the Soviet Union for twenty years, which, as Mikhail Ryklin justifiably points out, may have enhanced in him the East European penchant for idealization (the West as Intellectual Utopia, as discussed in the second chapter) during the Cold War era, "his idyllic vision of Western and especially French Culture" (Mikhail Ryklin, "Soznaniye kak prostranstvo svobody" [Conscience as the Realm of Freedom], afterword to *Soznaniye i tsivilizatsiya,* by Merab Mamardashvili (Moscow: Logos, 2004), 261.

5. Mamardashvili, "Evropeyskaya otvetstvennost'," 28.

6. Ibid., 26.

7. Alain Badiou, *The Century,* trans. Alberto Toscano (Cambridge: Polity Press, 2007), 9.

8. Giorgio Agamben, *The Open: Man and Animal,* trans. Kevin Attell (Stanford: Stanford University Press, 2004).

9. Gilbert Simondon, *Deux leçons sur l'animal et l'homme* (Paris: Ellipses, 2004), 9.

10. Agamben, *Open,* 38.

11. Ibid., 77.

12. Jean-Marie Schaeffer , *La Fin de l'exception humaine* (Paris: Gallimard, 2007).

13. Agamben, *Open*, 87.

14. Krzysztof Ziarek, "After Humanism: Agamben and Heidegger," *South Atlantic Quarterly* 8, no. 1 (2008): 187–209. The question of the human being with regard to the animal and the artificial creature certainly looms large: Suffice it to mention Donna Haraway's influential work (*Simians, Cyborgs, and Women*; *When Species Meet*) and the work on the animal that preoccupied Derrida in his last years (*The Animal That Therefore I Am*; *The Beast and the Sovereign*). While I find this problematic fascinating as a specific focus of research (see Miglena Nikolchina, "The Concave Mirror: Notes on the Parahuman in Kleist and Rilke" *Kritika i humanizîm*, no. 22 [2006]: 75–92), at this point I am interested in illustrating only yet another "vanishing" aspect of hetorotopian homonymy concerning a problem that is of crucial importance for the present epoch.

15. "The problem is always about free transformation or change. This is the problem of the event" (Merab Mamardashvili, *Strela poznaniya: Nabrosok yestestvenoistoricheskoy gnoseologii* [The Arrow of Knowledge: Toward the Gnoseology of Natural History] [Moscow: Shkola, 1996], 209).

16. Ibid., 293.

17. Merab Mamardashvili, *Vvedeniye v filosofiyi* [Introduction to Philosophy], in *Neobkhodimost' sebya: Doklady, stat'i, filosofskiye zametki* [The Necessity of Oneself: Speeches, Articles, Philosophical Notes], ed. Yu. P. Senokosov (Moscow: "Labirint," 1996). http://www.psylib.ukrweb.net/books/mamar02/index.htm.

18. Deyan Deyanov, "Posleslov. Mamardashvili i evropejskata filosofija na XX vek" [Afterword: Mamardashvili and Twentieth-Century European Philosophy], in *Izbrano*, by Merab Mamardashvili (Sofia: Iztok-Zapad, 2004), 353–74.

19. Mamardashvili, *Strela poznaniya*.

20. Annie Epelboin, "Merab Mamardashvili—grazhdanin mira," in *Uskol'zayushchiy kontekst: Russkaya filosofiya v postsovetskikh usloviyakh: Materialy konferentsii1* [Fleeing Context: Russian Philosophy in the Post-Soviet Situation], ed. Mikhail Ryklin et al. (Bremen, 1998). 188.

21. Ibid., 185.

22. See, for example, the story of Senokosov, the publisher of *The Arrow of Knowledge* (Yu. P. Senokosov, "Vmesto poslesloviya," in *Strela poznaniya: Nabrosok yestestvenoistoricheskoy gnoseologii*, by Merab Mamardashvili [Moscow: Shkola, 1996], 299–303), as well as Mikhail Ryklin, "Tsvety zapozdalyye: Metafizicheskaya tema u Meraba Mamardashvili" [Belated Flowers: The Problem of Meta-

physics in Merab Mamardashvili], in *Uskol'zayushchiy kontekst: Russkaya filosofiya v postsovetskikh usloviyakh: Materialy konferentsii* [Fleeing Context: Russian Philosophy in the Post-Soviet Situation], ed. Mikhail Ryklin et al. (Bremen, 1998), 191–207.

23. Ryklin, "Tsvety zapozdalyye."

24. Senokosov ("Vmesto poslesloviya") shares this view.

25. Hardly. Epelboin, for example, claims that Mamardashvili's French was impeccable and that he spoke French "like a poet" ("Merab Mamardashvili," 189).

26. Mamardashvili, "Evropeyskaya otvetstvennost'," 26.

27. Merab Mamardashvili, *Kantianskiye variatsii* [Kantian Variations] (Moscow: Agraf, 2002), 7.

28. Merab Mamardashvili, "Kartezianskiye razmyshleniya" [Cartesian Meditations], in *Filosofskiye chteniya* (St. Peterburg: Azbuka: Klasika, 2002), 508.

29. Mamardashvili, *Strela poznaniya*, 57.

30. Ibid., 38.

31. Mamardashvili, *Vvedeniye v filosofiyi.*

32. Mamardashvili, "Kartezianskiye razmyshleniya," 616.

33. Mamardashvili, *Strela poznaniya*,105.

34. Mamardashvili, *Vvedeniye v filosofiyi.*

35. Frank Pierobon, *L'Humanité tragique: Contribution à une phénoménologie de l'écriture* (Paris: Les éditions du cerf, 2008), 7–10.

36. Alenka Zupančič, *The Odd One In: On Comedy* (Cambridge, Mass.: MIT Press, 2008), 129.

37. On the transformation, in *Antigone*, of death from something that happens to us into a place see Alenka Zupančič, *The Shortest Shadow: Nietzsche's Philosophy of the Two* (Cambridge, Mass.: MIT Press, 2003), 171. On the mechanism of tragedy as incorporating (rather than repeating) a singular object see also Zupančič, *Odd One In*, 178.

38. A late and quite literal illustration of this process may be found in H. G. Wells's *The Island of Doctor Moreau* where the human is brutally inflicted through "vivisection" on the animal; the human is effected through "surgery" as a grim torture of the animal.

39. *Battlestar Galactica*, TV series, produced by David Eick et al., directed by Michael Rymer et al. (73 episodes), BSkyB/NBC, 2004–9, DVD.

40. This question is asked in *The Three Stigmata of Palmer Eldritch* (392—the italics are Dick's) but it clearly subtends the troubled effort

to define the *differentia specifica* of the human in *Do Androids Dream of Electric Sheep?* The movie *Blade Runner* was based on *Do Androids Dream of Electric Sheep?* with significant changes concerning many aspects of Dick's novel.

41. Jacques de Vaucanson (1709–1782), a French inventor who designed fascinating mechanisms and automata. Among the many thinkers who refer to him are Immanuel Kant and Julien de La Metrie, who significantly called him "a new Prometheus," a phrase that recurs during the eighteenth century and makes its way to the subtitle of *Frankenstein*.

42. Mladen Dolar, " 'I shall be with you on your wedding night': Lacan and the Uncanny," *October* 58 (Autumn 1991): 17.

43. http://starwars.wikia.com/wiki/Quote:C-3PO.

44. Zupančič, *Odd One In*, 132.

45. Once again, I rely on Mladen Dolar's ("The Aesthetics of the Uncanny"; "Comedy and Its Double"; " 'I shall be with you on your wedding night' ") and Alenka Zupančič's ("Comedy and the Uncanny"; "Ethics and Tragedy in Lacan"; *The Odd One In: On Comedy*) studies of the edge between the tragic, the comic, and the uncanny.

ADDENDUM: THE DISCRETIONS OF INVERTED THEORY

1. Mladen Dolar, " 'I shall be with you on your wedding night': Lacan and the Uncanny," *October* 58 (Autumn 1991): 13.

2. Tzotcho Boiadjiev, *"Nepisanoto uchenie" na Platon* [Plato's Unwritten Doctrine] (Sofia: Nauka i izkustvo, 1984), 20–21.

3. Tzotcho Boiadjiev, "Dialogichnijat printsip na istoriko-kulturnoto isledvane" [The Dialogical Principle of Historic Cultural Research], in *Avgustin i Dekart* [St. Augustine and Descartes] (Sofia: Sofia University Press, 1992), 112.

4. Ivaylo Ditchev, "The Transparent Book," In *Post-Theory, Games, and Discursive Resistance: The Bulgarian Case*, by Alexander Kiossev et al. (Albany: State University of New York Press, 1995), 1–2.

5. Julia Kristeva, *Desire in Language: A Semiotic Approach to Literature and Art*, trans. T. Gora, A. Jardine, and L. S. Roudiez (New York: Columbia University Press, 1980), 161.

6. Gayatri Chakravorty Spivak, *In Other Worlds, In Other Worlds: Essays In Cultural Politics* (New York: Routledge, 1988), 140.

7. Miglena Nikolchina, *Matricide in Language: Writing Theory in Kristeva and Woolf* (New York: Other Press, 2004), 45–61.

8. Julia Kristeva, *The Samurai*, trans. Barbara Bray (New York: Columbia University Press, 1992), 41.

9. Boyan Manchev, "Interpretatsii na ideologiata, ideologia na interpretatsiata: Vîrhu polemikite v bîlgarskoto literaturoznanie" [Interpretation of Ideology, Ideologies of Interpretation: On the Debates in Bulgarian Literary Theory], *Literaturna misîl*, no. 1 (1999): 5–30.

10. See Radosvet Kolarov, *Povtorenie i sutvorenie: Poetika na avtotekstualnosta* [Repetition and Creation: Poetics of Autotextuality] (Sofia: Prosveta, 2009), 220–27. It is impossible to trace here the transmodality of this very idea. One of the tracks could take us back to the 1960s and to Krassmir Mantchev's elaboration of Gustave Guillaume's concept of *idéogenèse*. See Krassmir Mantchev, "La hiérarchie sémantique des verbes français contemporains," *Cahiers de lexicologie*, no. 10 (1967): 31–46. See too Krassimir Mantchev, *Sémiotique et Narratologie* (Sofia: Presses Universitaires "St. Kliment Ohridski," 1998),121, and *Oeuvres complètes*, vol. 1: *La linguistique* (Paris, L'Harmattan, 2004), 193.

11. Kristeva, *Desire in Language*, vii.

12. The temptation of "literary or paraliterary fiction," which is resisted in the preface to *Desire in Language* (ix), turns into an *inescapable* "share of fiction" in *Powers of Horror: An Essay on Abjection*, trans. L. S. Roudiez (New York: Columbia University Press, 1982), 68). Later on her project is described as resembling "narrative fiction," as, ultimately, close to literature and art in its ambition to "restore to illusion its full therapeutic and epistemological value" (*In the Beginning was Love: Psychoanalysis and Faith*, trans. A. Goldhammer [New York: Columbia University Press, 1987], 21) and its cathartic effect (*Black Sun: Depression and Melancholia*, trans. L. S. Roudiez [New York: Columbia University Press, 1989], 35).

13. Maria Margaroni, "Julia Kristeva's Chiasmatic Journeys: From Byzantium to the Phantom of Europe and the End of the World," in *Psychoanalysis, Aesthetics, and Politics in the Work of Kristeva*, ed. Kelly Oliver and S. K. Keltner (Albany: State University Press of New York, 2009), 107–24.

14. Walter Benjamin, *The Origin of German Tragic Drama*, trans. J. Osborne (London: NLB, 1977), 178. See Nikolchina, *Matricide in Language*, 67.

15. Dylan Evans, *An Introductory Dictionary of Lacanian Psychoanalysis* (London: Routledge, 1996), 92.

16. Merab Mamardashvili, "Prevrashtenye formy (o neobhodymosti iratsional'nyh vyrazheniy)" [Inverted Forms: On the Necessity of Irrational Expressions], In *Kak ia ponimaiu filosofiu* [My Understanding of Philosophy] (Moscow: Progress, 1992), 269–82.

17. Kristeva, *Black Sun*, 4.

18. Julia Kristeva, *Murder in Byzantium*, trans. C. Jon Delogu (New York: Columbia University Press, 2006), 75.

19. Dusan I. Bjelic, "The Balkans and the 'History of Shit,'" *Eurozine*, http://www.eurozine.com/articles/2004-06-11-bjelic-en.html, accessed 22 March 2011.

20. "Today Philipopolis is a city like any city in Santa Varvara. . . . Since the fall of the Berlin wall Santa Varvara has expanded continuously" (Kristeva, *Murder in Byzantium*, 166). Philipopolis is the name given to the city by Philip of Macedon, the father of Alexander the Great. Using this name in this context rather than the modern name Plovdiv is indicative of the erasure of recent history subtending Kristeva's Byzantine utopia.

21. Ibid., 81.

22. Ibid., 67.

23. "Byzantium did not last, and France itself is fading" (ibid., 86).

24. In the novel, the crusader turns out to be the ancestor of Sebastian Chrest-Jones, a dark and obsessed murderous alter ego of Stephanie Delacour, who in her turn is Kristeva's alter ego, Chrest/Krist sound like the Bulgarian word for "cross" (*krîst*), which forms the root of Kristeva's family name. It is believed, indeed, that this rather common family name goes back to the crusaders, the ones "marked with a cross," many of whom did stay behind and left their traces in a number of toponyms in Bulgaria. The initials of Chrest-Jones reverse Julia Kristeva's initials (CJ/JK); Krist-Eva could be seen as the feminine of Chrest-Jones, etc. The novel is full of similar labyrinths that involve elements more complicated than sounds and names.

25. Kristeva, *Murder in Byzantium*, 123.

26. Vera Mutafchieva, *Az, Anna Comnina, Ritsariat* [I, Anna Comnena: The Knight], in *Selected Works* (Plovdiv: Zhanet-45, 2008), 3:52.

27. Ibid., 324.

28. *The Lives of Others*, film, directed by Florian Henckel von Donnersmarck (Arte, Bayerischer Rundfunk, 2006).

Works Cited

Agamben, Giorgio. *The Open: Man and Animal.* Translated by Kevin Attell. Stanford: Stanford University Press, 2004.

———. *The Time That Remains: A Commentary on the Letter to the Romans.* Translated by Patricia Dailey. Stanford: Stanford University Press, 2005.

Angelov, Angel. "Dialog i dialogizm" [Dialogue and Dialogism]. *Literaturen vestnik,* 9 April 1997.

Arendt, Hannah. *Between Past and Future: Eight Exercises in Political Thought.* Harmondsworth, Eng.: Penguin Books, 1977.

———. *The Human Condition.* Chicago: University of Chicago Press, 1958.

Badiou, Alain. *The Century.* Translated by Alberto Toscano. Cambridge: Polity Press, 2007.

———. *Infinite Thought: Truth and the Return to Philosophy.* Translated and edited by Oliver Feltham and Justin Clemens. London: Continuum, 2005.

———. *Theory of the Subject.* Translated by Bruno Bosteels. London: Continuum, 2009.

Battlestar Galactica. TV series. Produced by David Eick et al. Directed by Michael Rymer et al. 73 episodes. BSkyB/NBC, 2004–9. DVD.

Baumgartl, Bernd. *Transition and Sustainability: Actors and Interests in Eastern European Environmental Policies.* Boston: Kluwer Law International, 1997.

Beauvoir, Simone de. *The Second Sex.* Translated by H. M. Parshley. New York: Everyman's Library, 1993.

Benhabib, Seyla. *Situating the Self: Gender, Community, and Postmodernism in Contemporary Ethics.* New York: Routledge, 1992.

Benjamin, Walter. *The Origin of German Tragic Drama.* Translated by J. Osborne. London: NLB, 1977.

Bjelic, Dusan I. "The Balkans and the 'History of Shit.'" *Eurozine.* http://www.eurozine.com/articles/2004-06-11-bjelic-en.html, accessed 3/22/2011.

Blade Runner. Produced by Michael Deeley et al. Directed by Ridley Scott. Warner Bros., 1982. DVD.

Boiadjiev, Tzotcho. "Dialogichnijat printsip na istoriko-kulturnoto isledvane" [The Dialogical Principle of Historic Cultural Research]. In *Avgustin i Dekart* [St. Augustine and Descartes]. Sofia: Sofia University Press, 1992.

———. "Marsilio Ficino ili Eros kato krîgovrat na duha" [Marsilio Ficino or Eros as *Circuitus Spiritualis*]. In *Krîgovrat na duha,* 195–206. Sofia: LiK, 1998.

———. *"Nepisanoto uchenie" na Platon* [Plato's Unwritten Doctrine]. Sofia: Nauka i izkustvo, 1984.

———. "Predgovor" [Introduction] to *Filosofski Seminari: Gjolechitsa—20 Godini* [Philosophical Seminars: 20 Years After]. Sofia: Minerva, 2004.

Borges, Jorge Luis. "Mirrors." In *Selected Poems,* edited by Alexander Coleman. Harmondworth, Eng.: Penguin Books, 2000.

———. "Tlön, Uqbar, Orbis Tertius." In *Labyrinths: Selected Stories and Other Writings,* edited by Donald A. Yates and James E. Irby, 3–18. New York: New Directions, 1964.

Brossat, Alain, ed. *Michel Foucault: Les jeux de la verité et du pouvoir: Etudes transeuropéennes.* Nancy: Presses Universitaires de Nancy, 1994.

Brown, Wendy. *Edgework: Critical Essays on Knowledge and Politics.* Princeton: Princeton University Press, 2005.

———. *Politics Out of History.* Princeton: Princeton University Press, 2001.

———. *States of Injury: Power and Freedom in Late Modernity.* Princeton: Princeton University Press, 1995.

Buck-Morss, Susan. *Dreamworld and Catastrophe: The Passing of Mass Utopia in East and West.* Cambridge, Mass.: MIT Press, 2000.

———. "Pis'mo iz Nyu-Iorka" [A Letter from New York]. *Hudozhestvennyi zhurnal,* no. 25 (1999): 16–17.

Bundzhulov, Andrej. *Heterotopii.* Sofia: Kritika i humanizîm, 1995.

———. "Modernoto obshtestvo i socialisticheskata heterotopia" [Modern Society and the Socialist Heterotopia]. *Kritika i humanizîm* 3 (1991): 207–23.

———."Vlast i vidimost: Uvod vîv fenomenologiata na heliotorpizmite" [Power and Visibility: An Introduction to the Phenomenology of Heliotropisms]. *Kritika i humanizîm* 6 (1999): 161–76.

Busheikin, Laura. "I Don't Know What Feminism Is, but I Say NO." In *Butterbrod and Bodies,* 6–13. Prague: Center for Gender Studies, 1994.

Butler, Judith. *Bodies That Matter: On the Discursive Limits of "Sex."* New York: Routledge, 1993.

———. *Gender Trouble: Feminism and the Subversion of Identity.* New York: Routledge, 1990.

———. "Sex and Gender in Simone de Beauvoir's *Second Sex.*" *Yale French Studies* 72 (1986): 35–49.

———. *Undoing Gender.* New York: Routledge, 2004.

Copjec, Joan. "Sex and the Euthanasia of Reason." In *Read My Desire: Lacan against the Historicists.* Cambridge, Mass.: MIT Press, 1995.

Damyanova, Jana. "Protsesît na samotniya prelîstitel ili stradanieto na pisatelya ot podzemieto" [The Process/Trial of the Solitary Seducer; or, the Suffering of the Writer from the Underground]. In *Ars Erotica,* edited by Orlin Spasov, 66–88. Sofia: Institute for Children's Literature and Art, 1992.

Delbos, Victor. "Les Facteurs kantiens dans la philosophie allemande." *Revue de Métaphysique et de Morale* 23 (1925): 271–81.

Derrida, Jacques. *The Animal That Therefore I Am.* Translated by David Wills. New York: Fordham University Press, 2008.

———. *The Beast and the Sovereign.* Translated by Geoffrey Bennington. Chicago: University of Chicago Press, 2009.

———. "Différance." In *Margins of Philosophy,* translated by Alan Bass, 1–27. Chicago: University of Chicago Press, 1982.

———. "From Restricted to General Economy: A Hegelianism without Reserve." In *Writing and Difference,* translated by Alan Bass, 251–77. Chicago: University of Chicago Press, 1978.

———. *Positions*. Translated by Alan Bass. Chicago: University of Chicago Press, 1981.

———. "Qu'est-ce qu'une traduction 'relevante'?" In *Jacques Derrida*, edited by Marie-Louise Mallet and Ginette Michaud, 561–76. Paris: Éditions de l'Herne, 2004.

Deyanov, Deyan. "Filosofskoto inakomislie na Mamardashvili" [The Philosophical *Inakomislie* of Mamardashvili]. *Kritika i humanizîm* 6 (1999): 17–38.

———. "Neklasicheskata ratsionalnost kato problemno pole" [Nonclassical Rationality as a Problem Field]. *Kritika i humanizîm* 6 (1999): 5–6.

———. "Posleslov: Mamardashvili i evropejskata filosofija na XX vek" [Afterword: Mamardashvili and Twentieth-Century European Philosophy]. In *Izbrano*, by Merab Mamardashvili, 353–74. Sofia: Iztok-Zapad, 2004.

Deyanova, Lilyana. "Nevîzmozhnata kriticheska publichnost" [The Impossible Critical Publicity]. In *Medii i prehod* [Media and Transition], edited by Georgi Lozanov, Lilyana Deyanova, and Orlin Spasov, 240–56. Sofia: Center for Media Development, 2000.

Dick, Philip K. *Do Androids Dream of Electric Sheep?* In *Four Novels of the 1960s*, 431–608. New York: Library of America, 2007.

———. *The Three Stigmata of Palmer Eldritch*. In *Four Novels of the 1960s*, 231–430. New York: Library of America, 2007.

Ditchev, Ivaylo. *Donner sans perdre: L'échange dans l'imaginaire de la modernité*. Paris: Harmattan, 1997.

———. "Erotika na komunizma" [The Erotic of Communism]. In *Ars Erotica*, edited by Orlin Spasov, 153–60. Sofia: Institute for Children's Literature and Art, 1992.

———. "Literalisms." In *Post-Theory, Games, and Discursive Resistance: The Bulgarian Case,* by Alexander Kiossev et al., 3–9. Albany: State University of New York Press, 1995.

———. "The Transparent Book." In *Post-Theory, Games, and Discursive Resistance: The Bulgarian Case,* by Alexander Kiossev et al., 1–2. Albany: State University of New York Press, 1995.

Dolar, Mladen. "The Aesthetics of the Uncanny." *Mesotes: Zeitschrift für philosophischen Ost-West-Dialog* 3 (1991): 51–66.

———. "Comedy and Its Double." In *Schluss mit der Komödie!/Stop That Comedy!*, edited by Robert Pfaller, 181–210. Vienna: Sonderzahl, 2006.

———. "'I shall be with you on your wedding night': Lacan and the Uncanny." *October* 58 (Autumn 1991): 5–23.

Engelstein, Laura. "Culture, Culture Everywhere: Interpretations of Modern Russia, across the 1991 Divide." *Kritika: Explorations in Russian and Eurasian History* 2, no. 2 (2001): 363–93.

Epelboin, Annie. "Merab Mamardashvili—grazhdanin mira." In *Uskol'zayushchiy kontekst: Russkaya filosofiya v postsovetskikh usloviyakh: Materialy konferentsii*, edited by Mikhail Ryklin et al., 183–90. Bremen, 1998.

Evans, Dylan. *An Introductory Dictionary of Lacanian Psychoanalysis.* London: Routledge, 1996.

Florensky, P. A. "Perepiska" [Letters]. *Novyi mir,* no. 2 (1989): 194–203.

Foucault, Michel. *Fearless Speech.* Los Angeles: Semiotext(e), 2001.

———. "Les heterotopias." In *Die Heterotopien: Les heterotopias. Der utopische Körper. Le corps utopique*, 37–52. Frankfurt am Main: Suhrkamp, 2005.

———. "Of Other Spaces." *Diacritics* 16, no. 1 (1986): 22–27.

Fraser, Nancy. *Justice Interruptus: Critical Reflections on the "Postsocialist" Condition.* New York: Routledge, 1997.

Georgiev, Nikola. "Semeistvoto: nachin na upotreba" [The Family: How to Use It]. In *Nova kniga za bîlgarskiya narod* [The New Book of the Bulgarian People], 7–49. Sofia: Sofia University Press, 1991.

Goldfarb, Jeffrey C. "Why Is There No Feminism after Communism?" *Social Research: An International Quarterly of the Social Sciences* 64, no. 2 (1997): 236–57.

Goldsmith, Steven. "The Textual Logic of Democracy: Theory and the Crisis of Representation." In *The Ends of Theory,* edited by Jerry Herron, Dorothy Huson, Ross Pudaloff, and Robert Strozier, 135–45. Detroit: Wayne State University Press, 1996.

Haraway, Donna J. *Simians, Cyborgs, and Women: The Reinvention of Nature.* New York: Routledge, 1990.

———. *When Species Meet (Posthumanities).* Minneapolis: University of Minnesota Press, 2007.

Havel, Vaclav. *The Power of the Powerless: Citizens against the State in Central-Eastern Europe.* Edited by John Keane. New York: M. E. Sharpe, 1985.

Havelkova, Hana. "Transitory and Persistent Differences: Feminism East and West." In *Transitions,* edited by Scott, Kaplan, and Keates, 56–62.

Heer, Jeet. "Marxist Critics Are Following Me! How Philip K. Dick Betrayed His Academic Admirers to the FBI." *Lingua Franca* 11, no. 4 (2001): 26–31.

Hegel, G. W. F. *Sochinenija*. Moscow-Leningrad, 1934.

Hoffmann, E. T. A. "The Sandman." In *Fantastic Worlds*, edited by E. S. Rabkin, 214–46. Oxford: Oxford University Press, 1979.

Holquist, Michael. "Tsiolkovsky as a Moment in the Prehistory of the Avant-Garde." In *Laboratory of Dreams: The Russian Avant-Garde and Cultural Experiment*, edited by J. E. Bowlt and O. Matich, 100–117. Stanford: Stanford University Press, 1996.

Ilkov, Ani. *Izvorît na groznohubavite* [The Fountain of the Ugly Beauties]. Sofia: Anubis, 1994.

Inwood, Michael. *A Hegel Dictionary*. Oxford: Blackwell, 2003.

Jameson, Fredric. "Conversations on the New World Order." In *After the Fall: The Failure of Communism and the Future of Socialism*, edited by Robin Blackburn, 255–68. New York: Verso, 1991.

Jarczyk, Gwendoline, and Perre-Jean Labarrière. "Sursumer/ Sursomption." In *Hegeliana,* 102–20. Paris: Presses Universitaire de France, 1986.

Katsarska, Boryana. "Dusha. Eros. Obshtnost" [Soul. Eros. Community]. *Filosofski pregled* 2, no. 2 (1992): 3–14.

Kiossev, Alexander. "Golyamoto nedorazumenie: Zapad i iztok, paresiasti, filosofi, polititsi i medii v ikonomikata na istinata" [The Big Misunderstanding: West, East, Parrhesiasts, Philosophers, Politicians and the Media in the Economy of Truth]. In *Medii i mitove* [Media and Myths], edited by Georgi Lozanov and Orlin Spasov, 17–97. Sofia: Sofia University Press, 2000.

———. "Introduction: A Broken Promise." In *Post-Theory, Games, and Discursive Resistance: The Bulgarian Case*, edited by Alexander Kiossev et al., ix–xxi. Albany: State University of New York Press, 1995.

———. "Paranoia de la parrhesia." In *Michel Foucault: Les jeux de la verité et du pouvoir: Etudes transeuropéennes,* edited by Alain Brossat. Nancy: Presses Universitaires de Nancy, 1994.

Koev, Kolyo. "The Invisible Horizons of the Self-Evident." *Abstracts of the 8th International Congress of Logic, Methodology and Philosophy of Science*. Vol.5. Part 2. Moscow. 1987, 394-396.

Kojève, Alexandre. *Introduction à la lecture de Hegel*. Paris: Gallimard, 1947.

Kolarov, Radosvet. *Povtorenie i sutvorenie: Poetika na avtotekstualnosta* [*Repetition and Creation: Poetics of Autotextuality*]. Sofia: Prosveta, 2009.

Koyré, Alexandre. "Hegel à Iéna." In *Études d'histoire de la pensée philosophique*, 147–89. Paris: Gallimard, 1971.

———. "Note sur la langue et la terminologie hégelienne." In *Études d'histoire de la pensée philosophique*, 191–224. Paris: Gallimard, 1971.

———. "Rapport sur l'état des études hégeliennes en France." In *Études d'histoire de la pensée philosophique*, 225–49. Paris: Gallimard, 1971.

Kristeva, Julia. *Black Sun: Depression and Melancholia*. Translated by L. S. Roudiez. New York: Columbia University Press, 1989.

———. *Desire in Language: A Semiotic Approach to Literature and Art*. Translated by T. Gora, A. Jardine, and L. S. Roudiez. New York: Columbia University Press, 1980.

———. *In the Beginning Was Love: Psychoanalysis and Faith*. Translated by A. Goldhammer. New York: Columbia University Press, 1987.

———. *Murder in Byzantium*. Translated by C. Jon Delogu. New York: Columbia University Press, 2006.

———. *Powers of Horror: An Essay on Abjection*. Translated by L. S.Roudiez. New York: Columbia University Press, 1982.

———. *The Samurai*. Translated by Barbara Bray. New York: Columbia University Press, 1992.

Krushkova, Krasimira. "Ustnite kato kavichki" [The Lips as Quotation Marks]. In *Ars Erotica*, edited by Orlin Spasov, 95–99. Sofia: Institute for Children's Literature and Art, 1992.

Lacan, Jacques. *Écrits II*. Paris: Seuil, 1999.

———. "L'étourdit." In *Autres écrits*, 449–95. Paris: Le Seuil, 2001.

———. *Le Seminaire livre XX, Encore*. Paris: Seuil, 1975.

———. "The Signification of the Phallus." In *Feminine Sexuality: Jacques Lacan and the école freudienne*, edited by Juliet Mitchell and Jacqueline Rose, 74–85. New York: Norton, 1985.

Lawn, Victor H. "Satellite Rivals Sirius over City: New Yorkers Note Brilliance as They Get First View of an Artificial Moon." *New York Times*, 8 November 1957. http://www.nytimes.com/partners/aol/special/sputnik/sput-19.html.

Lem, Stanislaw. "The Mask." In *Mortal Engines*, translated and with an introduction by Michael Kandel, 181–239. San Diego: Harcourt Brace Jovanovich, 1992.

———. *Microworlds*. Edited by Franz Rottensteiner. San Diego: Harcourt Brace Jovanovich, 1984.

Lenin, V. I. "Detskaja bolezn' 'levizny' v kommunizme." *Polnoe sobranie*, vol. 41. Moscow: Izdatel'stvo politicheskoj literatury, 1981.

———. "Filosofskie tetrady." In *Polnoe sobranie, sochinenij*, 5-e izd., vol. 29. Moscow: Izdatel'stvo politicheskoj literatury, 1969.

———. "Gosudarstvo i revoljucija: Uchenie marksizma o gosudarstve i zadachi proletariata v revoljucii." In *Polnoe sobranie sochinenij*, 5-e izd., vol. 33. Moscow: Izdatel'stvo politicheskoj literatury, 1969.

Licheva, Amelia. "Golyamoto mîzhko priyatelstvo ili ima li neshto obshto mezhdu Robinzon Kruzo, Herman Hese i Aleksandîr Kyosev" [Sublime Male Bonding, or What Does Alexander Kiossev Have in Common with Robinson Crusoe and Herman Hesse]. *Kultura,* 10 July 1992.

Lotman, Yuri. *Kul'tura i vzryv* [Culture and Explosion]. Moscow: Gnozis, 1992.

———. "Sovremennost' mezhdu Vostokom i Zapadom" [The Present between East and West]. *Znamia,* no. 9 (1997): 157–62.

———. *Universe of the Mind: A Semiotic Theory of Culture*. Translated by A. Shukman. London: Tauris, 1990.

Malabou, Catharine. *La plasticité au soir de l'écriture: Dialectique, destruction, deconstruction*. Paris: Léo Scheer, 2005.

Mamardashvili, Merab. "Evropeyskaya otvetstvennost' " [The European Responsibility]. In *Soznaniye i tsivilizatsiya*, 26–29. Moscow: Logos, 2004.

———. *Kantianskiye variatsii* [Kantian Variations]. Moscow: Agraf, 2002.

———. "Kartezianskiye razmyshleniya" [Cartesian Meditations]. In *Filosofskiye chteniya*, 506–815. St. Petersburg: Azbuka: Klasika, 2002.

———. *Lektsii po antichnoi filosofii* [Lectures in Ancient Greek Philosophy]. Moscow: Agraf, 1997.

———. "Prevrashtenye formy (o neobhodymosti iratsional'nyh vyrazheniy)" [Inverted Forms: On the Necessity of Irrational Expressions]. In *Kak ia ponimaiu filosofiu* [My Understanding of Philosophy], 269–82. Moscow: Progress, 1992.

———. *Strela poznaniya: Nabrosok yestestvenoistoricheskoy gnoseologii* [The Arrow of Knowledge: Toward the Gnoseology of Natural History]. Moscow: Shkola, 1996.

———. *Vvedeniye v filosofiyi* [Introduction to Philosophy]. In *Neobkhodimost' sebya: Doklady, stat'i, filosofskiye zametki* [The Necessity of Oneself: Speeches, Articles, Philosophical Notes], edited by Yu. P. Senokosov. Moscow: "Labirint," 1996. http://www.psylib.ukrweb.net/books/mamar02/index.htm.

Manchev, Boyan. "Interpretatsii na ideologiata, ideologia na interpretatsiata: Vîrhu polemikite v bîlgarskoto literaturoznanie" [Interpretation of Ideology, Ideologies of Interpretation: On the Debates in Bulgarian Literary Theory]. *Literaturna misîl,* no.1 (1999): 5–30.

Mantchev, Krassimir. "La hiérarchie sémantique des verbes français contemporains." *Cahiers de lexicologie,* no. 10 (1967): 31-46.

———. *Oeuvres complètes.* Vol. 1: *La linguistique.* Paris: L'Harmattan, 2004.

———. *Sémiotique et Narratologie.* Sofia: Presses Universitaires "St. Kliment Ohridski," 1998.

Margaroni, Maria. "Julia Kristeva's Chiasmatic Journeys: From Byzantium to the Phantom of Europe and the End of the World." In *Psychoanalysis, Aesthetics, and Politics in the Work of Kristeva,* edited by Kelly Oliver and S. K. Keltner, 107–24. Albany: State University Press of New York, 2009.

Marody, Mira. "Why I Am Not a Feminist: Some Remarks on the Problem of Gender Identity in the United States and Poland." *Social Research: An International Quarterly of the Social Sciences* 60, no. 4 (1993): 853–64.

Miller-Pogacar, Anesa. "Introduction: Mikhail Epstein's Transcultural Visions." In *After the Future: The Paradoxes of Postmodernism and Contemporary Russian Culture,* by Mikhail N. Epstein, 1–16. Amherst: University of Massachusetts Press, 1995.

Mutafchieva, Vera. *Az, Anna Komnina: Ritsaryat* [I, Anna Comnena: The Knight]. In *Selected Works,* vol. 3. Plovdiv: Zhanet-45, 2008.

Nancy, Jean-Luc. *La remarque spéculative (un bon mot de Hegel).* Paris: Galilée, 1973.

Nikolchina, Miglena. "The Concave Mirror: Notes on the Parahuman in Kleist and Rilke." *Kritika i humanizîm,* no. 22 (2006): 75–92.

———. *Matricide in Language: Writing Theory in Kristeva and Woolf.* New York: Other Press, 2004.

———. "Postmodernata biblioteka" [The Postmodern Library]. In *I prochee* [Etcetera], edited by M. Abigar, V. Miteva, and H. Todorov, 95–105. Sofia: Sofia University Press, 1990.

Nikolova, Nina. "Politanatomiya na moderniya chovek" [Political Anatomy of the Modern Human Being]. *Kritika i humanizîm* 3 (1991): 91–109.

Petrova, Dimitrina. "Bulgaria." In *Dissent and Opposition in Communist Eastern Europe: Origins of Civil Society and Democratic Transition*, edited by D. Pollack and J. W. Aldershot, 161–82. London: Ashgate, 2004.

Petrovskaia, Elena. "Jetot smutnyj obraz devjanostyh" [The Murky Image of the Nineties]. *Hudozhestvennyj Zhurnal*, no. 25 (1999): 13–15.

Philmus, Robert. "The Two Faces of Philip K. Dick." *Science Fiction Studies* 18, no. 1 (1991): 91–103.

Pierobon, Frank. *L'Humanité tragique: Contribution à une phénoménologie de l'écriture*. Paris: Les éditions du cerf, 2008.

Popov, Julian. "'Za nas kinoto e nai-vazhnoto izkustvo'" [For Us Cinema Is the Most Important Art]. In *Ars Erotica*, edited by Orlin Spasov, 172–76. Sofia: Institute for Children's Literature and Art, 1992.

Raichev, Andrei. "Migratsionnite obshtestva i vtorata mrezha" [The Migration Societies and the Second Network]. *Kritika i humanizîm* 3 (1991): 195–204.

Rickman, Gregg. "Dick, Deception, and Dissociation: A Comment on 'The Two Faces of Philip K. Dick.'" *Science Fiction Studies* 18, no. 2 (1991): 290–93.

Rivière, Joan. "Womanliness as a Masquerade." In *Formations of Fantasy*, edited by Victor Burgin, James Donald, and Cora Kaplan, 35–44. New York: Methuen, 1986.

Rooney, Ellen. "A Semiprivate Room." *Differences: A Journal of Feminist Cultural Studies* 13, no. 1 (2002): 128–56.

Ryklin, Mikhail. "Parnikovyi effect" [The Greenhouse Effect]. 1994. http://azbuka.gif.ru/critics/parnik/.

———. "Soznaniye kak prostranstvo svobody" [Conscience as the Realm of Freedom]. Afterword to *Soznaniye i tsivilizatsiya*, by Merab Mamardashvili, 259–67. Moscow: Logos, 2004.

———. "Tsvety zapozdalyye: Metafizicheskaya tema u Meraba Mamardashvili" [Belated Flowers: The Problem of Metaphysics in Merab Mamardashvili]. In *Uskol'zayushchiy kontekst: Russkaya filosofiya v postsovetskikh usloviyakh: Materialy konferentsii* [Fleeing Context: Russian Philosophy in the Post-Soviet Situation], edited by Mikhail Ryklin et al., 191–207. Bremen, 1998.

Salecl, Renata. *The Spoils of Freedom: Psychonalaysis and Feminism after the Fall of Socialism*. New York: Routledge, 1994.

Saunders, Frances Stonor. "Modern Art Was CIA 'Weapon': Revealed: How the Spy Agency Used Unwitting Artists such as Pollock and de Kooning in a Cultural Cold War." *Independent,* 22 October 1995.

Schaeffer, Jean-Marie. *La Fin de l'exception humaine*. Paris: Gallimard, 2007.

Scott, Joan W. "Fantasy Echo: History and the Construction of Identity." *Critical Inquiry* 27 (2001): 284–304.

———. "Fictitious Unities: 'Gender,' 'East' and 'West.'" Fourth Feminist Research Conference, Bologna, September 2000. http://www.women.it/cyberarchive/files/scott.htm

———. *Only Paradoxes to Offer: French Feminists and the Rights of Man*. Cambridge, Mass.: Harvard University Press, 1996.

Scott, Joan, Cora Kaplan, and Debra Keates, eds. *Transitions, Environments, Translations: Feminism in International Politics*. New York: Routledge, 1997.

Senokosov, Yu. P. "Vmesto poslesloviya." In *Strela poznaniya: Nabrosok yestestvenoistoricheskoy gnoseologii*, by Merab Mamardashvili, 299–303. Moscow: Shkola, 1996.

Sharp, Joanne P. "Gendering Nationhood: A Feminist Engagement with National Identity." In *Body Space: Destabilizing Geographies of Gender and Sexuality*, edited by Nancy Duncan, 97–108. New York: Routledge, 1996.

Siklova, Jirina. "Feminism and the Roots of Apathy in the Czech Republic." *Social Research: An International Quarterly of the Social Sciences* 64, no. 2 (1997): 258–80.

———. "McDonalds, Terminators, Coca Cola Ads, and Feminism?" In *Bodies of Bread and Butter: Reconfiguring Women's Lives in Post-Communist Czech Republic*, edited by Susana Trnka and Laura Busheikin, 7–11. Prague: Prague Gender Center, 1993.

Simondon, Gilbert. *Deux leçons sur l'animal et l'homme*. Paris: Ellipses, 2004.

Spivak, Gayatri Chakravorty. *In Other Worlds: Essays In Cultural Politics*. New York: Routledge, 1988.

Stambolova, Albena. "Pisane i prelîstyavane" [Writing and Seduction]. In *Ars Erotica*, edited by Orlin Spasov, 60–65. Sofia: Institute for Children's Literature and Art, 1992.

Stanev, Ivan. *Lapsus Linguae: Theaterstücke, Theoretische Lähmungen, Ontologische Gesänge.* Berlin: Autoren Kollegium, 1992.

———. "Predstavlenie i nakazanie" [Performance and Punishment]. In *Izbitite obitateli: Poeziya, drama, teoriya: Iz tetradkite na edin zakîsnyal modernist* [The Slaughtered Tenants: Poetry, Drama, Theory: From the Notebooks of a Belated Modernist], 89–134. Sofia: Virga, 1994.

Stoyanov, Tzvetan. "Za hubavite razgovori" [On Good Conversations]. In *Kulturata kato obshtenie* [Culture as Communication], 67–71. Sofia: Bulgarski pisatel, 1988.

Subeva, Svetlana. "Kîm kriticheskata istoriya na modernata publichnost" [Toward the Critical History of Modern Publicity]. *Kritika i humanism* 3 (1991): 111–22.

Sumin, Oleg. *Gegel' kak sud'ba Rossii* [Hegel as the Destiny of Russia]. Sofia: Malvina, 1997.

Todorov, Vladislav. "The Conquest of the Vacuum." Manuscript. No date.

———. "Eros, Ritsariat na protezata" [Eros, the Knight of the Prosthesis]. In *Ars Erotica*, edited by Orlin Spasov, 219–53. Sofia: Institute for Children's Literature and Art, 1992.

———. *Red Square/Black Square: Organon for Revolutionary Imagination*. Albany: State University of New York Press, 1995.

———. "Teror i terorizîm" [Terror and Terrorism]. In *Medii i mitove* [Media and Myths], edited by Georgi Lozanov and Orlin Spasov, 250–59. Sofia: Sofia University Press, 2000.

Treneva, Simona. "Za edna alternative na ofitsialnata bulgarska sotsiologia v kraia na 70te i prez 80te godini na 20 vek" [Toward an Alternative of the Official Bulgarian Sociology from the End of the 1970s and during the 1980s]. *Sotsiologicheski problemi* 37, no. 3–4 (2005): 287–301.

Vattimo, Gianni. *The Transparent Society.* Translated by David Webb. Cambridge: Polity Press, 1992.

Vernadsky, Vladimir. "Neskol'ko slov o noosfere" [A Few Words about the Noosphere]. In *Russkii kosmizm: Antologia filosofskoi mysli*, edited by A. G. Gacheva and S. G. Semyonova, 303–11. Moscow: Pedagogika-Press, 1993.

Vernant, Jean-Pierre. "Mamardashvili, chovekît na slovoto" [Mamardashvili, the Man of the Word]. *Kultura,* 1 December 2000.

Volodin, A. I. *Gegel' i russkaja socialisticheskaja mysl' XIX veka* [Hegel and Russian Nineteenth-Century Socialist Thinking]. Moscow: Mysl', 1973.

Wahl, Jean. "Le role de A. Koyré dans le developpement des études hegeliennes en France." *Hegel-Studien*, Beiheft, 3 (1966): 15–26.

Watson, Peggy. "Civil Society and the Politics of Difference in Eastern Europe." In *Transitions*, edited by Scott, Kaplan, and Keates, 21–29.

———. "Rethinking Transition: Globalism, Gender, and Class." *International Feminist Journal of Politics* 2, no. 2 (2000): 185–213.

———. "The Rise of Masculinism in Eastern Europe." *New Left Review* 198 (1993): 71–82.

Yanakiev, Kalin. "Vsekidnevniyat svyat na srednovekovniya chovek: Eros i distantsiya" [The Everyday Life of the Medieval Person: Eros and Distance]. In *Ars Erotica*, edited by Orlin Spasov, 19–33. Sofia: Institute for Children's Literature and Art, 1992.

Zdravomyslova, Elena, and Anna Temkina. "Social'noe konstruktirovanie gendera kak feministkaya teoriya" [The Social Construction of Gender as Feminist Theory]. In *Zhenshchina, gender, kultura* [Woman, Gender, and Culture], 61–62. Moscow: MZGI, 1999.

Ziarek, Krzysztof. "After Humanism: Agamben and Heidegger." *South Atlantic Quarterly* 8, no. 1 (2008): 187–209.

Žižek, Slavoj. *The Parallax View*. Cambridge, Mass.: MIT Press, 2006.

———. "A Plea for Leninist Intolerance." *Critical Inquiry* 28 (2002): 542–66.

Zupančič, Alenka. "Comedy and the Uncanny." In *Why Psychoanalysis?* 59–75. Uppsala: NSU Press, 2008.

———. "Ethics and Tragedy in Lacan." In *The Cambridge Companion to Lacan*, edited by Jean-Michel Rabaté, 173–90. Cambridge: Cambridge University Press, 2003.

———. *The Odd One In: On Comedy*. Cambridge, Mass.: MIT Press, 2008.

———. *The Shortest Shadow: Nietzsche's Philosophy of the Two*. Cambridge, Mass.: MIT Press, 2003.

Index